HOW TO MAKE **BREAD**

RYLAND PETERS & SMALL
LONDON • NEW YORK

HOW TO MAKE BREAD

Step-by-step recipes for yeasted breads,
sourdoughs, soda breads and pastries

EMMANUEL HADJIANDREOU   photography by Steve Painter

DEDICATION
For my supportive and loving wife Lisa, my
gorgeous boy Noah Elliot and my mum, Elena,
who has guided me through my life.

**Design, Photographic Art Direction
  and Prop Styling** Steve Painter
Senior Editor Céline Hughes
Production Controller Toby Marshall
Art Director Leslie Harrington
Publishing Director Alison Starling

US Recipe Tester Susan Stuck
Indexer Hilary Bird

First published in 2011
by Ryland Peters & Small
20–21 Jockey's Fields
London WC1R 4BW
and
341 E 116th St
New York, NY 10029

www.rylandpeters.com

20 19 18 17 16 15 14 13 12 11

Text © Emmanuel Hadjiandreou 2011
Design and photographs
© Ryland Peters & Small 2011

ISBN 978 1 84975 140 7

A catalogue record for this book is available from the
British Library.

Library of Congress Cataloging-in-Publication Data

Hadjiandreou, Emmanuel.
 How to make bread : step-by-step recipes for yeasted
breads, sourdoughs, soda breads and pastries /
Emmanuel Hadjiandreou ; photography by Steve Painter.
      p. cm.
 Includes index.
 ISBN 978-1-84975-140-7
 1. Bread. 2. Cookbooks. I. Title.
 TX769.H225 2011
 641.81'5—dc23
                                   2011025873

Printed and bound in China

Notes
• All spoon measurements are level, unless otherwise
specified.
• Ovens should be preheated to the specified
temperature. Recipes in this book were tested using a
fan/convection oven. If using a regular oven, follow the
manufacturer's instructions for adjusting temperatures.
• All eggs are medium, unless otherwise specified.
Recipes containing raw or partially cooked egg should not
be served to the very young, very old, anyone with a
compromised immune system or pregnant women.

CONTENTS

INTRODUCTION

Ever since I can remember, baking has been an important part of my life. There was a great food influence in my life with my father owning and running restaurants with his brother while I was young. This allowed me to be introduced to new and exciting flavours and has helped me to be innovative in my baking now.

Bread is special – from the moment you start mixing the ingredients to the time when you take it out of the oven, tap it on the bottom to check for a hollow sound and then that unmistakable smell that overwhelms you as the baked bread cools. It is quite magical.

I have never tired of making bread. No matter how many loaves I have had to produce or what the challenge has been, I have jumped in with my heart and soul and created each and every loaf with the same amount of passion I would put into creating only one.

After gaining my apprenticeship and qualifications in German-style bakeries in South Africa and Namibia, I worked and travelled with my wife Lisa, building and learning new techniques and recipes in Greece and Germany. I was taught to produce large quantities of bread as well as individual showpieces without sacrificing quality or consistency.

On arriving in the UK, my baking world exploded! I met and worked with incredibly passionate and like-minded artisans. My hunger for learning, developing and creating new loaves took over. I was very fortunate to be able to use the best organic and natural ingredients available and to work in the most wonderful environments.

Through my years of baking and running bakeries, I have had enormous pleasure in introducing apprentices and young bakers to my world of bread and inspiring them to become successful, enthusiastic and knowledgeable bakers. Through teaching, which is what I mostly do now, I get as much joy in seeing my students learn how to achieve a great loaf as I do with baking it myself.

This book is an accumulation of the recipes I have developed through my baking life, so they have been thoroughly tried, tested and enjoyed. My ultimate goal has always been to make bread with a deep, satisfying flavour and a good crust. From the basic recipes to the more exciting and interesting sourdough processes, this book will guide you on your baking adventure. I believe that everyone can make a loaf of bread, and with practice, it can be great bread.

FLOUR AND SALT

Flour can be made from different grains. Most of the flour used in this book is made from wheat or rye.

Each grain of wheat contains three main elements: bran, endosperm and germ. The way in which the wheat is milled determines which parts of the grain remain in the flour, and which are lost. There are two ways of making flour from wheat.

1 Stoneground flour is obtained by crushing the wheat between two millstones. The resulting flour is considered wholemeal or whole-wheat and generally retains all three parts of the grain. When this flour is sifted and therefore refined, white flour is obtained. It is normally grey because there are trace elements of bran that can't be removed.

2 Roller-milled flour is made using a series of metal rollers that crush the grain to a powder. Roller-milled flour is generally broken down into its different parts, then put back together. White flour is normally roller milled. If you buy a bag of wheat flour, unless it is specifically labelled stoneground, it has been roller milled.

Wholemeal/whole-wheat flour contains 100% of the original grain and therefore nothing has been destroyed or lost during milling.

When flour and water are mixed, the starch in the flour absorbs the water and, as a result, some of the starch is converted to sugar. Yeast feeds off the sugar and produces carbon dioxide. The combination of flour, water and kneading helps to create gluten, which is responsible for the elasticity of bread dough. Gluten traps carbon dioxide thereby ensuring that the bread rises and creates the little bubbles you see in a slice of baked bread.

WHEAT FLOURS

Many varieties of wheat are grown and a miller will blend different varieties to make different types of white flour. For example, **plain white or all-purpose flour** has a medium protein (and therefore gluten) content – about 10%. It contains 75% of the original grain, which means that most of the bran and germ have been removed. It is mainly used for baking cookies, pastries and some cakes. **Cake flour or soft flour** has an even lower protein content (about 8%) and a high starch content.

For bread making, we require strong/bread flour. **Strong or bread flour** is specially blended by the miller for bread making and it contains a high amount of protein (up to 17%) to trap the carbon dioxide during fermentation and give the bread a good texture. Look for organic or unbleached flour for the best results. Other grades of flour include brown and white wholemeal/whole-wheat.

In the UK, **malthouse or Granary-style flour** is a brown flour containing malted grain. Malting is a process whereby a grain is allowed to start germinating – during which starch is converted to sugar – and then roasted. The malted grain is either added whole to flour or it is ground first and mixed into the flour. The resulting bread is sweeter and nuttier than other breads. Where this flour cannot be found, a blend can be made (see page 19).

Self-raising/self-rising flour has had baking powder added to it. It is used in cake making.

In France and Germany, flour is named after the ash content in the flour. The higher the number, the higher the protein content and the greater the percentage of original grain. French flours range from Type 45 to T150. In Germany, the numbers range from 450 to 1600. In Italy, the flour is classified by how finely it is ground, starting from *tipo* "1", through "0" and "00", which is powdery soft.

RYE FLOUR

With a lower gluten content than wheat, rye flour by itself makes a dense loaf of bread. It is high in fibre, minerals and antioxidants, and can usually be found as light, medium or dark rye flour, depending on the amount of bran remaining. Dark rye flour is sometimes called pumpernickel flour in the USA.

SPELT FLOUR

Spelt is an ancient grain, known variously as Roman wheat, *dinkel* in Germany and *farro* in Italy. It can usually be found as white or wholegrain flour. It is high in fibre and protein, and is more easily digested than wheat, so is suitable for the wheat-intolerant.

KHORASAN OR KAMUT FLOUR

Khorasan is an ancient grain, known as Egyptian wheat. It is high in protein and tends to be suitable for the wheat-intolerant. You will most likely find it sold under the trade name of Kamut.

SALT

Salt is very important in the bread-making process. Not only does it season the bread but it also reacts with the protein in the flour to strengthen the gluten, and it deepens the colour of the bread crust. It is also a preservative, helping to prolong the bread's shelf life. However, too much salt can prevent the bread from rising.

YEAST AND WATER

Yeast is a single-celled fungus. As I mentioned on page 8, yeast feeds on sugar to produce carbon dioxide as well as a small amount of alcohol. This is a type of fermentation and is very important both because of its ability to make bread rise but also to give flavour to the bread. In this book we will be using three kinds of yeast: fresh yeast, dried/active dry yeast and sourdough starter (see opposite), which you will make yourself.

TYPES OF YEAST

Fresh compressed yeast comes in block form (called 'cakes') and should always be beige and crumbly or putty-like. If exposed to air for a long period of time, it will oxidize and darken. Discard any dark bits and use the rest as soon as possible. Always refrigerate fresh yeast in an airtight container or wrapped in clingfilm/plastic wrap. Dried/active dry yeast needs to be dissolved in water before use. (Instant or rapid-rise yeast is mixed directly into flour: it is not used in these recipes.) Once opened it should be kept in a sealed container. The recipes in this book use fresh yeast or dried/active dry yeast, but I highly recommend fresh if you can find it. You only ever need half the weight of dried yeast as fresh. Check expiration dates before using.

WATER

Water helps yeast to rise and promote gluten, which is present in the flour. It is important to use room temperature or warm water as stated in the recipes. Warm water should feel like blood temperature when you put your finger in it. In areas where water is very hard or strongly chlorinated, use bottled spring water. As a rule, in all the recipes in the book I always dissolve the yeast in water before starting the bread-making process.

SOURDOUGH

Wheat, rye and other grains have been combined with water by bakers for thousands of years to make sourdough starters. Wild yeast spores are present in air and flour. Mixing flour and water and allowing it to ferment – ie when yeast breeds and produces carbon dioxide – creates a starter (also known as the 'chef' or 'mother'). The starter takes 3–5 days to develop and, when it is ready, can be used (in place of baker's yeast) to make bread.

Day 1: Mix 1 teaspoon flour and 2 teaspoons water in a clear jar. Seal and let stand overnight.

Days 2, 3, 4 and 5: Add 1 teaspoon flour and 2 teaspoons water to the jar and stir. More and more bubbles will form on the surface.

To make a starter, mix 15 g/1 tablespoon from the jar with 150 g/1 generous cup flour and 150 g/150 ml/⅔ cup warm water in a large bowl. Cover and let ferment overnight. The next day, use the amount of starter needed for your recipe.

Add 1 teaspoon flour to the remaining ferment in the jar, seal and refrigerate for use another time. If it is left in the refrigerator for a long time, it might become dormant. Throw away the acidic liquid on the surface, stir in 30 g/2 tablespoons flour and 30 g/30 ml/2 tablespoons water, mix to a paste, seal and let stand overnight. The next day, if bubbles have formed, it is ready to be made into a starter. If not, repeat the process above. Treat your sourdough with tender loving care and you can keep it indefinitely.

day 1   day 2   day 3   day 4   day 5

TOOLS AND EQUIPMENT

Accuracy is crucial in bread making. For this reason, I have given all ingredients in metric weights first (including salt, yeast and liquids), followed by American cups and/or ounces, teaspoons or tablespoons. I highly recommend that you weigh everything on high-precision electronic scales, but of course it's up to you. A properly measured cup of white flour weighs 120 g or 4¼ oz. When measuring flour by the cup, spoon it into the appropriate measuring cup and scrape off the excess in a clear glass or acrylic measuring cup with a pour spout and a handle.

Precision electronic scales: See paragraph above. If you choose to weigh your bread-making ingredients (rather than measure them in cups and spoons), you want scales that can weigh between 1 g and about 3 kg. They tend to come in 1-g, 2-g or 5-g graduation, so make sure you buy scales with a 1-g graduation for the most accurate measurement of ingredients like yeast, salt and water.

At least 1 large mixing bowl (approximately 2-litre/8-cup capacity) and **at least 1 small mixing bowl (approximately 1-litre/4-cup capacity):** You want to be able to fit one bowl on top of the other snugly. You can either upturn the smaller one and put it inside the bigger bowl; or you can upturn the larger one and place it over the smaller one. I find this the most convenient way to mix wet and dry ingredients, as well as providing an easy covering while the dough rises. I normally use a plastic or Pyrex bowl, but if you use Pyrex, make sure you rinse the bowl in warm water to warm it up if it has been stored in a cold cupboard.

Roasting pan: You will need to put a cup of water in this to create steam in your oven. Put the pan on the bottom of the oven before preheating it.

Loaf pans: 500-g/6 x 4-inch (or 1-lb.) and 900-g/8½ x 4½-inch (or 2-lb.) capacities are what we mainly use in this book.

Proofing/dough-rising baskets: These come in various shapes and sizes and are used to hold dough during proofing. They shape the dough and create attractive patterns on the crust of the baked bread. They are made from a variety of materials. These baskets are not essential to bread making but are a good investment for the avid baker.

Proofing/baker's linen (couche) or clean tea/kitchen towel: This is a thick linen traditionally used to support dough inside a proofing basket (especially French baguettes) and also to absorb a little moisture from the dough, which helps to form the bread crust. You can also use thick, heavy, clean tea/kitchen towels for this and to cover the dough during proofing.

Baking stone: Avid bakers might like to invest in a baking stone. Baking stones come in a variety of materials and thicknesses, and are designed to help bake bread evenly. They should be put in the oven and preheated slowly at the same time as the oven. If you put a cold stone in a very hot oven, it can crack. See also 'baking sheets' below.

Bread or pizza peel: Use this to slide the bread into the hot oven.

Baking sheets: You will often need more than one baking sheet if you are making individual pastries or similar. See also 'baking stone' above.

Metal dough scraper or **sharp, serrated knife:** A metal dough scraper makes dividing dough accurate and easy, but a sharp, serrated knife works well, too.

Plastic dough scraper: This scrapes dough and stray ingredients cleanly from the edge of a mixing bowl so that all the ingredients are well incorporated.

Lamé: This is a small, very sharp blade like a scalpel to score and slash the surface of the bread before baking. You can use a clean razor blade securely attached to the end of a wooden coffee stirrer (see photograph on page 52) or a small, very sharp knife instead.

As well as the more specialist pieces of equipment above, you will also need many of these common kitchen items.

Chopping/cutting board
Clingfilm/plastic wrap or a clean plastic bag
Fine sieve/strainer or flour sifter
Kitchen timer
Large knife
Measuring jug or cups
Measuring spoons
Non-stick parchment paper
Pair of kitchen scissors
Pastry brush
Rolling pin
Round cake pans
Saucepans
Slotted spoon
Wire rack for cooling
Wooden spoon

GUIDELINES AND TIPS

GETTING STARTED

1 The most important thing is to check that you have all the ingredients you need and in the right quantities. There is nothing worse than going straight into a recipe and getting halfway through before you realize that you have the wrong type of flour, your yeast has passed its expiration date or you don't have enough oats.

2 Start by clearing your work surface.

3 Measure all the ingredients and have them ready in front of you. Some recipes list the same ingredient twice, in different quantities. This is because, for example, 125 g/1 cup strong/bread flour is needed for one step of the recipe and then an additional 250 g/ 2 cups is needed later. Make sure you have taken this into account when you are checking you have enough flour in your cupboard.

4 Read the recipe all the way through and make sure you have all the appropriate equipment ready, including bowls, containers and/or baking pans. Only specific baking pans and special bread-making equipment (such as proofing/dough-rising baskets and baking sheets lined with parchment paper) are itemized in individual recipes. You should assume that each recipe will require other basic kitchen equipment, as listed on page 13.

5 When a recipe states that it makes a small loaf, this is equivalent to one made in a 500-g/6 x 4-inch loaf pan, from which you will get about 12 slices; if a large loaf, this equates to a 900-g/8½ x 4½-inch loaf pan or about 21 slices.

MAKING AND KNEADING THE DOUGH

1 Make sure the dry ingredients are well mixed before proceeding with the recipe.

2 Make sure the yeast is completely dissolved before proceeding with the recipe.

3 Recipes usually advise you to mix the dry ingredients into the wet ingredients so that you can use the bowl that had the dry ingredients to cover the mixture. I find this a very good system, so that's what I've advised for most recipes in this book.

4 Mix everything together very well. You could start doing this with a wooden spoon, then continue with your hands when the mixture comes together to form a dough.

5 You might like to use a plastic dough scraper to scrape the side of the bowl and the wooden spoon, and make sure you have mixed in all the dough into a ball, ready to rest.

6 Now cover with the bowl that had the dry mixture in it. Place it upside down over the bowl with the dough. This provides a tight, neat covering, but if you prefer, you can wrap the bowl in a clean, clear plastic bag that you have blown up. Avoid using clingfilm/plastic wrap because the dough can get stuck to it when it rises.

7 Let the dough rest for the time stated in the recipe – usually 10 minutes. During this time, gluten will start to form (see page 8).

8 After resting, the dough requires kneading in order to strengthen and promote the gluten. I believe in a very basic method of kneading: see page 20 for instructions and step-by-step pictures showing you how to do this. The dough is effectively folded inside the mixing bowl 10 times and for about 10 seconds. No lengthy pummelling or pounding, or indeed elbow grease, is needed!

9 We do this 10-second kneading process 4 times in total, with 10 minutes of rest between each stage. I always make a small indentation in the dough each time I knead it to keep track of how many stages of kneading it has been through. You will see these dents in the dough in some of the pictures throughout the book.

10 After the 4 stages of kneading, cover the dough again (as in Step 6) and let rest for 1 hour to ferment and develop flavour. Covering the bowl will ensure that a skin doesn't form on the dough.

SHAPING

1 After 1 hour, the rested dough is uncovered. You will notice an alcoholic smell coming from the dough; this is the by-product of fermentation. There should also be signs of moisture on the bowl or plastic bag that was covering the dough.

2 The dough will have risen substantially, so gently punch it down with your fist to deflate it.

3 Sprinkle a little flour (whichever flour you are using for the recipe) over a clean work surface, remove the dough from the bowl and place it on the floured surface.

4 If the dough is sticky, sprinkle a little flour on it and/or on your hands to stop it sticking.

5 Using your hands, shape the dough into a ball, a flattened oval, a loaf shape or whichever shape is described in the recipe.

6 Instructions for shaping dough in the recipes may sometimes seem complicated or laborious, but the dough needs to be handled and shaped in such a way as to maximize gluten development and ensure the dough rises evenly while baking.

7 If you are making more than one item, divide the dough into equal portions using a metal dough scraper or sharp, serrated knife. I usually weigh each portion and add or subtract dough from each one until they all weigh the same. This ensures that all the portions bake evenly.

8 If you find that the dough is contracting or the surface is cracking while you are shaping it, cover and let rest for 5 minutes.

9 Place the dough(s) on a baking sheet lined with parchment paper, a floured or cloth-lined proofing/dough-rising basket or in the greased loaf pan, as instructed in the recipe.

PROOFING/RISING

1 Now the bread is ready to proof (or rise). The best conditions for proofing are warmth and slight humidity, so you will need to cover the dough.

2 I recommend that you turn your oven into a 'proofer'. To do this, preheat the oven to its very lowest setting (50°C or 120°F). Now turn the oven off: **this is very important**. Slide a rack in the middle and put a clean, wet tea/kitchen towel on the rack. Place the bread for proofing/rising in the warm oven on the tea/kitchen towel and let it rise. Check the bread from time to time and, once it has nearly doubled in volume, remove the bread and the towel and preheat the oven to the required temperature, ready for baking.

3 If you do not want to use your oven in this way, cover the bread with an upside-down bowl or wrap the bowl in a clean, clear plastic bag and blow it up. Place a cup of boiling water nearby. The cup of water in this step and the towel in Step 2 will provide the humidity and warmth necessary for the dough to rise.

4 Proofing/rising is very important because it encourages the yeast to multiply, resulting in a light, risen loaf.

SLASHING

1 When the bread has finished proofing/rising, you may like to slash the top to create a pattern and also to allow gas to escape as the loaf bakes.

2 For slashing, you can either use a lamé (see page 13), a clean razor blade securely attached to the end of a wooden coffee stirrer or a small, very sharp knife.

3 Always score just the surface of the loaf – don't cut too deeply – and it helps to hold the lamé or knife at a 45° angle to the surface of the bread.

BAKING

1 For most recipes, you will need to preheat the oven to its highest setting – 240°C (475°F) Gas 9 using the fan setting, if possible. If there is no fan setting, select the setting that heats the oven from top and bottom.

2 Always give the oven time to reach the required temperature. Ovens vary, but generally speaking, you will need 20–30 minutes to attain the highest temperature.

3 Make sure you have a rack in the middle of the oven on which to place the bread if it is in a loaf pan.

4 Put a deep roasting pan in the bottom of the oven.

5 Prepare a cup of water and set aside. This will create steam.

6 If you are using a baking stone, place this on the middle rack of the oven to preheat. Never put a cold baking stone in a hot oven because the sudden change in temperature can make it crack.

7 When the bread is ready to go in the oven, if it is in a loaf pan, slide onto the middle rack in the oven and immediately pour the reserved cupful of water into the hot roasting pan at the bottom.

8 If the loaf has been in a proofing/dough-rising basket, transfer it to a floured bread peel, and then slide it onto your preheated baking stone. If you're not using a baking stone, transfer the bread straight to a paper-lined baking sheet and slide onto the middle rack in the oven. Remember to pour the reserved cupful of water into the hot roasting pan at the bottom.

9 Steam is important for many reasons. When the bread is put in the oven, it starts to bake from the outside in. If there is no steam, you will get a poor colour and the surface of the bread can crack. However, steam helps to glaze the bread and soften the crust, letting out the air bubbles so that the surface does not crack. And where it is slashed, the incision is more pronounced. You also get a better colour and crust.

10 Always bake the bread in a properly preheated oven and remember to lower the temperature if stated.

11 If the bread is browning too much, lower the oven temperature and cover the surface with a sheet of parchment paper.

12 To check if it is baked through, tip the bread out of the loaf pan or tip it over and tap the bottom – it should sound hollow.

13 If it is not ready, return to the oven for a few minutes.

14 If it is ready, set it on a wire rack to cool.

15 Always remember that hot bread, when taken out of the oven, continues to bake, and the crust will seem very doughy for up to 15 minutes.

BASICS & OTHER YEASTED BREADS

SIMPLE WHITE BREAD
WITH TWO VARIATIONS

This is the recipe that I suggest you start with on your bread-making adventure. It is the blueprint for most recipes in this book. The variations are made in exactly the same way, but be aware that malthouse flour can be hard to find, so use the blend suggested below.

WHITE

300 g/2½ cups white strong/bread flour

6 g/1 teaspoon salt

3 g fresh yeast or 2 g/¾ teaspoon dried/active dry yeast

200 g/200 ml/¾ cup warm water

500-g/6 x 4-in. loaf pan, greased with vegetable oil

MAKES 1 SMALL LOAF

MALTHOUSE

300 g/2½ cups malthouse flour (or 1½ cups unbleached bread flour, ⅔ cup multigrain blend or medium rye flour and ⅓ cup malted wheat flakes)

6 g/1 teaspoon salt

3 g fresh yeast or 2 g/¾ teaspoon dried/active dry yeast

200 g/200 ml/¾ cup warm water

WHOLEMEAL/WHOLE-WHEAT

300 g/2½ cups stoneground wholemeal/whole-wheat flour

6 g/1 teaspoon salt

3 g fresh yeast or 2 g/¾ teaspoon dried/active dry yeast

230 g/230 ml/1 scant cup warm water

1 In one (smaller) mixing bowl, mix the flour and salt together and set aside. This is the dry mixture. **(A)**

2 In another (larger) mixing bowl, weigh out the yeast. **(B)**

3 Add the water to the yeast. **(C)**

4 Stir until the yeast has dissolved. This is the wet mixture. **(D)**

5 Add the dry mixture to the wet mixture. **(E)**

6 Mix the mixtures together with a wooden spoon and then your hands until they come together to form a dough. **(F)**

7 Use a plastic scraper to scrape the side of the bowl clean and make sure all the ingredients are thoroughly mixed. **(G)**

8 Cover with the bowl that had the dry mixture in it. **(H)**

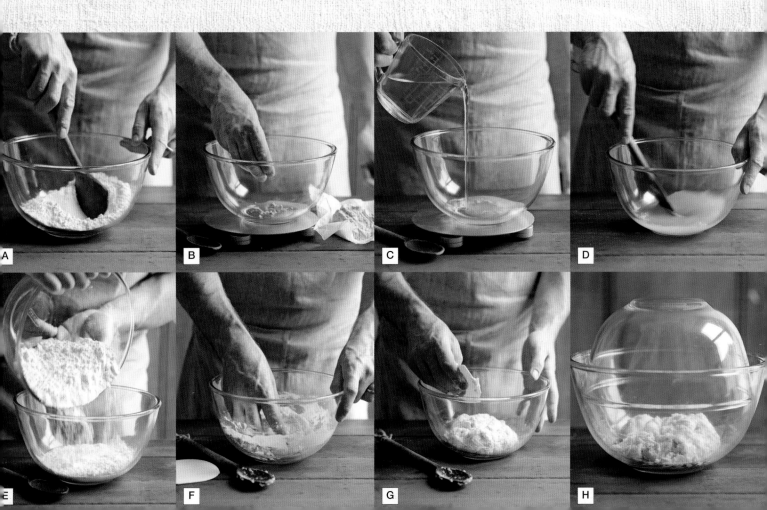

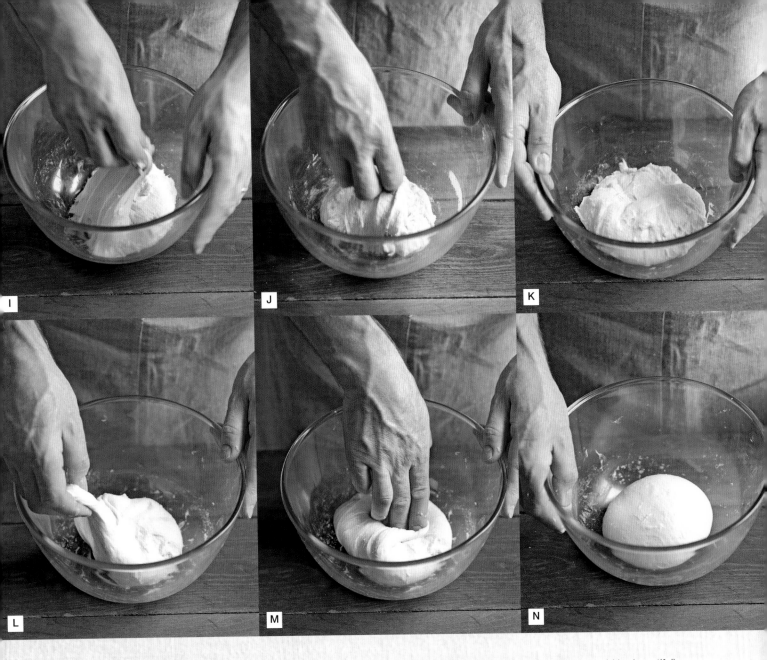

9 Let stand for 10 minutes.

10 After 10 minutes, the dough is ready to be kneaded. Leaving it in the bowl, pull a portion of the dough up from the side and press it into the middle. Turn the bowl slightly and repeat this process with another portion of dough. Repeat another 8 times. The whole process should only take about 10 seconds and the dough should start to resist. (I) (J) (K)

11 Cover the bowl again and let stand for 10 minutes.

12 Now repeat Steps 10 and 11 twice. After the second kneading, the dough should resist strongly when you pull it. (L)

13 After the third kneading, the dough should be beautifully smooth. (M)

14 Repeat Step 10 one last time.

15 After the fourth kneading, you should have a smooth ball of dough when you turn it over in the bowl. (N)

16 Now cover the bowl again and let rise for 1 hour.

17 When the dough has doubled in volume, punch it down gently with your fist to release the air. (O)

18 Lightly dust a clean work surface with flour.

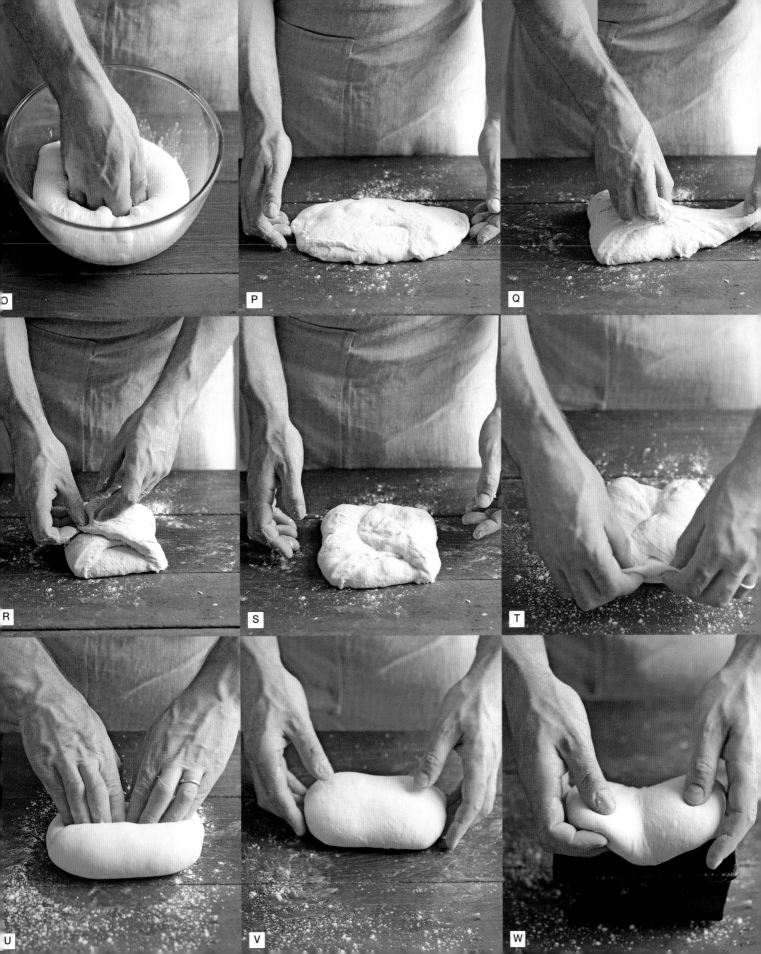

X

Y

Z

AA

19 Remove the ball of dough from the bowl and place it on the floured work surface. Gently flatten the dough into an oval. **(P)**

20 Fold the right end of the oval over into the middle. **(Q)**

21 Now fold the left end of the oval over to the middle. **(R)**

22 Press down slightly to seal the dough together. You will now have a roughly rectangular shape. **(S)**

23 Now you can start to shape the dough into a loaf: pull and fold the top of the rectangle one third of the way toward the middle, pressing it into the dough. **(T) (U)**

24 Swivel the dough 180° and then repeat Step 22. Repeat until you have a neat, reasonably flat loaf shape roughly the size of your loaf pan. **(V)**

25 Place the dough inside the prepared loaf pan, seam-side down. **(W)**

(X) shows this simple white bread plus the malthouse and wholemeal/whole-wheat variations in their pans.

26 Cover the loaf pan with the large bowl or a clean plastic bag (blown up) and let rise until slightly less than double the size – about 30–45 minutes.

27 About 20 minutes before baking, preheat the oven to 240°C (475°F) Gas 9 (fan setting, if possible) or as high as your oven will go. Place a roasting pan at the bottom of the oven to preheat. Fill a cup with water and set aside.

28 When the dough has finished rising, remove the bowl or covering. **(Y)**

29 Place the loaf in the preheated oven, pour the reserved cupful of water onto the hot roasting pan to form steam and lower the oven temperature to 200°C (400°F) Gas 6.

30 Bake for about 35 minutes, or until golden brown. **(Z)**

31 To check if it is baked through, tip it out of the pan and tap the bottom – it should sound hollow. **(AA)**

32 If it is not ready, return to the oven for a few minutes. If it is ready, set it on a wire rack to cool. **(BB)**

A

B

C

BREAD ROLLS

Bread rolls are a great alternative to sliced bread for sandwiches and they also make the best burger buns.

200 g/1½ cups white strong/bread flour

4 g/¾ teaspoon salt

6 g fresh yeast or 3 g/1 teaspoon dried/active dry yeast

130 g/130 ml/½ cup warm water

baking sheet lined with parchment paper

MAKES 4 ROLLS

1 Make the Simple White Bread dough using the ingredients given here, but following the instructions on pages 19–23 up to the end of Step 19.

2 Divide the dough into 4 equal portions using a metal dough scraper or sharp, serrated knife. **(A)**

3 Each portion should weigh about 80 g/2½–3 oz. If you want to be as accurate as possible, weigh each piece and add or subtract dough from the portions until they all weigh the same.

4 Take one portion of dough and roll between your hands until you get a perfectly round, smooth ball. Flatten one side slightly and lay it, flat-side down, on the prepared baking sheet. Repeat with the remaining dough. **(B)**

5 Cover the rolls with a large bowl. **(C)**

6 Let rise until slightly less than double the size – about 15–20 minutes.

7 Meanwhile, preheat the oven to 240°C (475°F) Gas 9 (fan setting, if possible) or as high as your oven will go. Place a roasting pan at the bottom of the oven to preheat. Fill a cup with water and set aside.

8 When the rolls have finished rising, remove the bowl covering them.

9 Place the rolls in the preheated oven, pour the reserved cupful of water onto the hot roasting pan to form steam and lower the oven temperature to 200°C (400°F) Gas 6.

10 Bake the rolls for about 15 minutes, or until golden brown.

11 To check if they are baked through, turn one roll over and tap the bottom – it should sound hollow.

12 If they are not ready, return to the oven for a few minutes. If they are ready, set on a wire rack to cool.

A

B

PLAIN SODA BREAD

250 g/2 cups white
strong/bread flour or
wholemeal/Irish-style
wholemeal flour

6 g/1 teaspoon salt

4 g/1 teaspoon
bicarbonate of/baking
soda

260 g/260 ml/1 cup plus
1 tablespoon whole
milk or buttermilk

*1 pie dish/plate,
greased with vegetable
oil, or 1 baking sheet
lined with parchment
paper*

**MAKES 1 SMALL
BREAD**

This is the simplest of breads, requiring no yeast and no rising, and you can make it with white or wholemeal flour, depending on your preference. The trick is to make the dough swiftly, with the minimum of mixing, and then to bake it as fast as possible. I recommend that you enjoy it fresh and warm with butter and, if possible, homemade jam.

1 Preheat the oven to 200°C (400°F) Gas 6.

2 In a mixing bowl, mix the flour, salt and bicarbonate of/baking soda together and set aside. This is the dry mixture.

3 Pour the milk or buttermilk into the dry mixture. Mix until it just comes together. Do not overmix. **(A)**

4 Lightly dust a clean work surface with flour.

5 Transfer the dough to the floured work surface.

6 Shape the dough into a ball and flatten slightly. Roll generously in white or wholemeal flour.

7 Slash a deep cross over the bread using a sharp, serrated knife. **(B: shows one bread made with white flour and one made with wholemeal flour)**

8 Place into a prepared pie dish/plate or on the prepared baking sheet.

9 Bake in the preheated oven for 20–30 minutes, or until baked through. To check if they are baked through, tip one upside down and tap the bottom – it should sound hollow.

10 If they are not ready, return to the oven for a few minutes. If they are ready, set on a wire rack to cool.

WHOLEGRAIN FRUIT SODA BREAD

I created this at Daylesford Organic as a twist on plain soda bread. It has an interesting texture and is sweetened by the dried fruit, making it perfect for breakfast. You will need to start the recipe a day in advance.

125 g/1 cup chopped/
cracked wheat or
wheat flakes

50 g/½ cup sultanas/
golden raisins

125 g/125 ml/½ cup
whole milk

freshly squeezed juice
and grated zest of
1 lemon

125 g/1 cup wholemeal/
Irish-style wholemeal or
white whole-wheat flour

3 g/½ teaspoon salt

3 g/¾ teaspoon
bicarbonate of soda/
baking soda

*baking sheet lined with
parchment paper*

MAKES 1 SMALL BREAD

1 In one (larger) mixing bowl, mix the chopped/cracked wheat or wheat flakes, sultanas/golden raisins, milk and lemon juice and zest. This is the wet mixture.

2 Cover by putting a smaller mixing bowl upside down over it. Refrigerate overnight.

3 The next day, preheat the oven to 200°C (400°F) Gas 6.

4 Take the wet mixture out of the refrigerator. Remove the smaller bowl from the top and mix the flour, salt and bicarbonate of/baking soda in it. This is the dry mixture.

5 Add the dry mixture to the wet mixture and mix with a wooden spoon until it all comes together. **(A)**

6 If the mixture is too dry and does not come together, add a little milk.

7 Lightly dust a clean work surface with flour.

8 Remove the dough from the bowl and place it on the floured work surface. Sprinkle some wholemeal flour over it. **(B)**

9 Shape the dough into a ball and sprinkle more flour generously over it. **(C)**

10 Flatten the bread slightly and slash a deep cross over it using a sharp, serrated knife. **(D)**

11 Place the ball of dough on the prepared baking sheet.

12 Bake in the preheated oven for 20–30 minutes, or until baked through. To check if it is baked through, tip it upside down and tap the bottom – it should sound hollow.

13 If it is not ready, return to the oven for a few minutes. If it is ready, set it on a wire rack to cool.

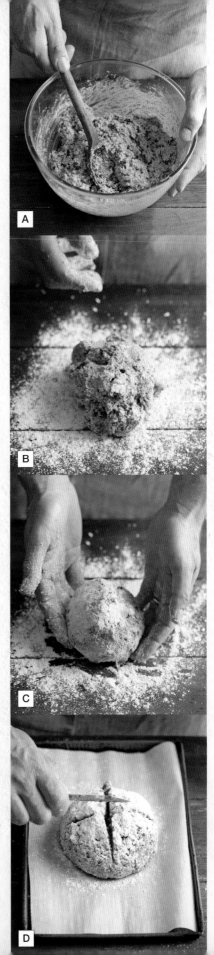

A

B

C

D

29

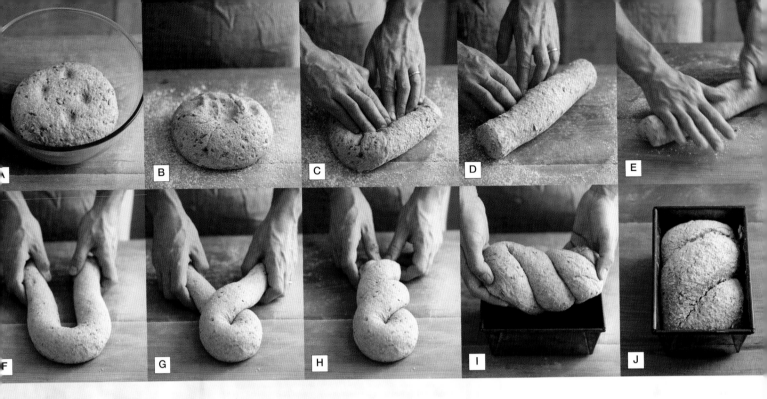

MULTIGRAIN SEEDED BREAD

This wholesome bread tastes wonderfully nutty thanks to the variety of seeds. One slice is so hearty and packed with flavour that it will keep you feeling full for a long while!

300 g/300 ml/1¼ cups cold water

20 g/2 tablespoons sesame seeds

20 g/2 tablespoons linseed/flaxseed

20 g/2 tablespoons buckwheat grain or kasha (roasted buckwheat)

20 g/2 tablespoons sunflower seeds, lightly toasted (optional)

500 g/4 cups wholemeal/whole-wheat flour

10 g/2 teaspoons salt

8 g fresh yeast or 4 g/1¼ teaspoons dried/active dry yeast

80 g/80 ml/⅓ cup warm water

900-g/8½ x 4½-in. loaf pan, greased with vegetable oil

MAKES 1 LARGE LOAF

1 Put the 300 g/300 ml/1¼ cups water and seeds in a (larger) mixing bowl and stir. This is the wet mixture. Cover by putting a smaller mixing bowl upside down over it. Set aside in a cool place overnight.

2 The next day, take the wet mixture out of the refrigerator. Remove the smaller bowl from the top and mix the flour and salt in it. This is the dry mixture.

3 In another small bowl, weigh out the yeast. Add the 80 g/80 ml/⅓ cup water and stir until the yeast has dissolved.

4 Mix the yeast solution into the wet mixture, then add the dry mixture and mix by hand until it comes together. Cover with the bowl that had the dry mixture in it. Let stand for 10 minutes.

5 Knead the dough as in Step 10 on page 23.

6 Cover the bowl again and let stand for 10 minutes.

7 Repeat Steps 5 and 6 twice, then Step 5 again. Cover the bowl again and let rise for 1 hour. **(A)**

8 Punch down the dough.

9 Lightly dust a clean work surface with flour. Put the dough on the work surface. Fold one edge of the dough over into the middle. Fold the opposite edge over to the middle. **(B) (C)**

10 Now roll the dough to make a sausage about twice the length of the loaf pan. **(D) (E)**

11 Shape the sausage into an inverted 'U'. **(F)**

12 Twist the 2 strands until you reach the end, then place inside the prepared loaf pan. **(G) (H) (I)**

13 Sprinkle flour over the bread. Cover and let rise until double the size – about 45 minutes. **(J)**

14 About 20 minutes before baking, preheat the oven to 240°C (475°F) Gas 9. Place a roasting pan at the bottom of the oven. Fill a cup with water.

15 Place the risen bread in the preheated oven. Pour the reserved cupful of water onto the hot roasting pan and lower the temperature to 220°C (425°F) Gas 7. Bake for about 30 minutes, or until golden brown. To check if it is baked through, tip it out of the pan and tap the bottom – it should sound hollow.

PIZZA DOUGH

This recipe makes five individual bases. After rolling out the dough into bases, bake for about 10 minutes or until beginning to colour, then let cool, wrap in clingfilm/plastic wrap and freeze for another time. When ready, let thaw, apply toppings and bake until golden.

500 g/4 cups white strong/bread flour

10 g/2 teaspoons salt

2 g fresh yeast or 1 g/ ¼ teaspoon dried/active dry yeast

250 g/250 ml/1 cup warm water

toppings of your choice, eg mozzarella, fresh sage, drizzle of olive oil and sea salt

parchment paper

baking sheet

baking stone and floured bread/pizza peel (optional)

MAKES 5 PIZZA BASES

1 In one (smaller) mixing bowl, mix the flour and salt together and set aside. This is the dry mixture.

2 In another (larger) mixing bowl, weigh out the yeast. Add the water to the yeast. Stir until the yeast has dissolved. This is the wet mixture.

3 Add the dry mixture to the wet mixture.

4 Mix the mixtures together with a wooden spoon and then your hands until they come together to form a dough.

5 Cover with the bowl that had the dry mixture in it.

6 Let stand for 10 minutes.

7 Knead the dough as in Step 10 on page 20.

8 Cover the bowl again and let stand for 10 minutes.

9 Repeat Steps 7 and 8 twice, then Step 7 again.

10 Cover the bowl again and let rise in a cool place for 24 hours.

11 The next day when the dough has doubled in volume, punch it down with your fist to release the air.

12 Lightly dust a clean work surface with flour.

13 Remove the ball of dough from the bowl and place it on the floured work surface. Divide it into 5 equal portions using a metal dough scraper or sharp, serrated knife.

14 Take one portion of dough and roll between your hands until you get a perfectly round, smooth ball. Flatten one side slightly and lay it, flat-side down, on the work surface. Repeat with the remaining portions of dough. **(A)**

15 Cover the balls of dough with a large bowl. Let rest for 10 minutes.

16 Roll out each ball of dough with a rolling pin until as thin as you like. **(B)**

17 Prick the bases all over with a fork. **(C)**

18 Lay each base on a sheet of parchment paper and arrange the toppings of your choice over the top, then let rest for 10–15 minutes.

19 Meanwhile, preheat the oven to 240°C (475°F) Gas 9. Set a baking sheet or baking stone in the oven to preheat. Place a roasting pan at the bottom of the oven. Fill a cup with water and set aside.

20 Slide a pizza base onto the floured bread/pizza peel, if using. **(D)**

21 Transfer the pizza base to the preheated baking sheet or stone, pour the reserved cupful of water onto the hot roasting pan to form steam and lower the oven temperature to 220°C (425°F) Gas 7.

22 Bake for about 15 minutes, or until golden brown. Bake the remaining bases individually.

A   B   C   D

CIABATTA

This popular Italian bread is named after its characteristic appearance, *ciabatta* being the Italian word for 'slipper'. Time and patience (and olive oil!) are needed to create those lovely bubbles in the loaf. It is best warm, dipped in olive oil and balsamic vinegar or slathered with butter.

A

B

C

200 g/1½ cups white strong/bread flour or Italian "00" flour

4 g/¾ teaspoon salt

2 g fresh yeast or 1 g/¼ teaspoon dried/active dry yeast

150 g/150 ml/⅔ cup warm water

about 50 g/50 ml/3 tablespoons olive oil

baking sheet lined with parchment paper

MAKES 2 SMALL CIABATTAS

1 In one (smaller) mixing bowl, mix the flour and salt together and set aside. This is the dry mixture.

2 In another (larger) mixing bowl, weigh out the yeast. Add the water and stir until the yeast has dissolved. This is the wet mixture.

3 Add the dry mixture to the wet mixture.

4 Mix the mixtures together with a wooden spoon until you get a fairly sticky dough.

5 Put about one third of the olive oil in another large mixing bowl and place the sticky dough in it.

6 Cover and let rest for 1 hour.

7 After 1 hour, gently fold the dough twice.

8 Cover with the bowl that had the dry mixture in it.

9 Now repeat Steps 6–8 three times, adding a little olive oil before resting the dough each time so that it does not stick too much to the bottom of the bowl.

10 At the very end of the resting cycle, the dough should be well risen and bubbly.

11 Dust a clean work surface well with flour.

12 Transfer the dough to the floured work surface. Be gentle so that you do not damage the air bubbles. **(A)**

13 Divide the dough into 2 equal portions using a metal dough scraper or sharp, serrated knife.

14 If you want to be as accurate as possible, weigh both pieces and add or subtract dough until they weigh the same.

15 Apply flour to your hands, then use to roughly mould each portion of dough into a slipper shape. Roll each ciabatta in flour. **(B)**

16 Place the ciabattas on the prepared baking sheet. **(C)**

17 Let rest for 5–10 minutes.

18 Meanwhile, preheat the oven to 240°C (475°F) Gas 9.

19 Bake the ciabattas in the preheated oven for about 15 minutes, or until golden brown. (You do not need a cupful of water in the bottom of the oven to create steam here because ciabatta dough is moist enough to create its own steam.)

20 To check if the ciabattas are baked through, tip upside down and tap the bottom – it should sound hollow.

21 If they are not ready, return to the oven briefly. (Do not bake for too long – ciabatta should be very soft on the inside with only a thin crust.) If they are ready, set on a wire rack to cool.

A

B

C

D

FOCACCIA

Focaccia is made with the same dough as ciabatta, but can then be used as a base for some delicious toppings. Tear into chunks and enjoy at a picnic or on a long car trip.

200 g/1½ cups white strong/bread flour or Italian "00" flour

4 g/¾ teaspoon salt

2 g fresh yeast or 1 g/¼ teaspoon dried/active dry yeast

150 g/150 ml/⅔ cup warm water

about 50 g/50 ml/ 3 tablespoons olive oil, plus extra to drizzle

toppings of your choice, eg fresh rosemary sprigs and coarse sea salt; or thinly sliced red onion and pieces of cooked potato; or pitted Kalamata olives; or halved cherry tomatoes and half-dried tomatoes

baking sheet lined with parchment paper

MAKES 1 FOCACCIA

1 In one (smaller) mixing bowl, mix the flour and salt together and set aside. This is the dry mixture.

2 In another (larger) mixing bowl, weigh out the yeast. Add the water and stir until the yeast has dissolved. This is the wet mixture.

3 Add the dry mixture to the wet mixture.

4 Mix the mixtures together with a wooden spoon until you get a fairly sticky dough.

5 Put about one third of the olive oil in another large mixing bowl and place the sticky dough in it. **(A)**

6 Cover and let rest for 1 hour.

7 After 1 hour, gently fold the dough twice. **(B)**

8 Cover with the bowl that had the dry mixture in it.

9 Now repeat Steps 6–8 three times, adding a little olive oil before resting the dough each time so that it does not stick too much to the bowl.

10 At the very end of the resting cycle, the dough should be well risen and bubbly. **(C)**

11 Transfer the dough to the prepared baking sheet. Be gentle so that you do not damage the air bubbles.

12 Cover and let rest for 10 minutes.

13 Push the dough out with your fingertips to flatten it and widen it into a rough square. **(D)**

14 Cover and let rest for 10 minutes.

15 Arrange the toppings of your choice over the top of the focaccia, pressing them into the dough slightly. If you are using olives, arrange them over one half of the focaccia, then fold over and press lightly. This will prevent the olives from burning in the oven. Drizzle olive oil lightly over the toppings. **(E) (F) (G) (H)**

16 Cover and let rise until about doubled in volume – about 20 minutes.

17 Meanwhile, preheat the oven to 240°C (475°F) Gas 9.

18 Bake the focaccia in the preheated oven for about 15–20 minutes, or until golden brown. (You do not need a cupful of water in the bottom of the oven to create steam here because focaccia dough is moist enough to create its own steam.)

19 To check if the focaccia is baked through, tip it upside down and tap the bottom – it should sound hollow.

20 If it is not ready, return to the oven briefly. If it is ready, set it on a wire rack to cool.

E   F   G   H

OLIVE AND HERB BREAD

Olives have always been a big part of my life – my father is Greek and he still salts and cures olives where he lives in Greece. They give a great flavour to bread.

40 g/¼ cup green pitted olives or green olives stuffed with pimento

40 g/¼ cup black pitted olives

1 teaspoon mixed dried herbs, eg herbes de Provence

250 g/2 cups white strong/bread flour

4 g/¾ teaspoon salt

3 g fresh yeast or 2 g/¾ teaspoon dried/active dry yeast

180 g/180 ml/¾ cup warm water

baking sheet lined with parchment paper

MAKES 1 SMALL LOAF

1 Mix the olives with the herbs and set aside.

2 In one (smaller) mixing bowl, mix the flour and salt together and set aside. This is the dry mixture.

3 In another (larger) mixing bowl, weigh out the yeast. Add the water and stir until the yeast has dissolved. This is the wet mixture.

4 Add the dry mixture to the wet mixture.

5 Mix the mixtures together with a wooden spoon and then your hands until they come together to form a dough.

6 Cover with the bowl that had the dry mixture in it.

7 Let stand for 10 minutes.

8 After 10 minutes, add the olive mixture to the dough. Knead gently as in Step 10 on page 20 until the olive mixture is thoroughly incorporated.

9 Cover the bowl again and let stand for 10 minutes.

10 Repeat Steps 8 and 9 twice, then Step 8 again. Cover the bowl again and let rise for 1 hour.

11 When the dough has doubled in volume, punch it down with your fist to release the air. **(A)**

12 Lightly dust a clean work surface with flour.

13 Remove the ball of dough from the bowl and place it on the floured work surface. Gently pull it into a long rectangle. **(B)**

14 Fold the left-hand third of the rectangle over toward the right. **(C)**

15 Now fold the right-hand third over. **(D)**

16 Press down slightly to seal the dough together. You will now have a neat rectangular loaf shape.

17 Turn the loaf over and place on the prepared baking sheet. Dust with flour. **(E)**

18 Cover the loaf and let rise until slightly less than double the size – about 30–45 minutes.

19 About 20 minutes before baking, preheat the oven to 240°C (475°F) Gas 9. Place a roasting pan at the bottom of the oven to preheat. Fill a cup with water and set aside.

20 When the dough has finished rising, remove the bowl or covering.

21 Place the loaf in the preheated oven, pour the reserved cupful of water onto the hot roasting pan and lower the oven temperature to 200°C (400°F) Gas 6.

22 Bake the bread for about 35 minutes, or until golden brown.

23 To check if the bread is baked through, tip it upside down and tap the bottom – it should sound hollow.

24 If it is not ready, return to the oven for a few minutes. If it is ready, set it on a wire rack to cool.

A   B   C   D   E

250 g/2 cups malthouse flour (or 1 cup unbleached bread flour, ⅔ cup multigrain blend or medium rye flour and ⅓ cup malted wheat flakes)

6 g/1 teaspoon salt

75 g/¾ cup chopped walnuts

3 g fresh yeast or 2 g/¾ teaspoon dried/active dry yeast

180 g/180 ml/¾ cup warm water

baking sheet lined with parchment paper

MAKES 1 SMALL LOAF

WALNUT BREAD

Walnuts always add a wonderful flavour to bread and instantly make it perfect with cheese or just as a bit of luxury at the weekend.

1 In one (smaller) mixing bowl, mix the flour, salt and walnuts together and set aside. This is the dry mixture.

2 In another (larger) mixing bowl, weigh out the yeast. Add the water and stir until the yeast has dissolved. This is the wet mixture.

3 Add the dry mixture to the wet mixture and mix with a wooden spoon and then your hands until they come together to form a dough.

A

B

C

D

E

F

4 Cover with the bowl that had the dry mixture in it.

5 Let stand for 10 minutes.

6 After 10 minutes, knead the dough as in Step 10 on page 20.

7 Cover the bowl again and let stand for 10 minutes.

8 Repeat Steps 6 and 7 twice, then Step 6 again. Cover the bowl again with the bowl that had the dry mixture in it or a clean plastic bag (blown up) and let rise for 1 hour.

9 Make sure you cover the dough with a bowl or plastic bag, not a towel, otherwise a skin will form on the dough. **(A)**

10 Punch down the dough with your fist to release the air. Lightly dust a clean work surface with flour.

11 Remove the ball of dough from the bowl and place it on the floured work surface. Shape it into a ball with your hands. **(B)**

12 Flatten it gently into a neat, rounded disc, then push your index finger through the middle to make a hole. **(C)**

13 Enlarge the hole slightly. Now place the dough ring onto the prepared baking sheet. **(D)**

14 Cover the bread again and let rise until slightly less than double the size – about 30–45 minutes.

15 About 20 minutes before baking, preheat the oven to 240°C (475°F) Gas 9. Place a roasting pan at the bottom of the oven to preheat. Fill a cup with water and set aside.

16 When the dough has finished rising, remove the bowl or covering. Dust with flour. **(E)**

17 Slash a large square over the bread using a sharp, serrated knife. **(F)**

18 Place the bread in the preheated oven, pour the reserved cupful of water onto the hot roasting pan and lower the oven temperature to 200°C (400°F) Gas 6.

19 Bake for about 30 minutes, or until brown.

20 To check if the bread is baked through, tip it upside down and tap the bottom – it should sound hollow.

21 If it is not ready, return to the oven for a few minutes. If it is ready, set it on a wire rack to cool.

PECAN RAISIN BREAD

Pecan and sultana is another combination that works so well in bread. This is a recipe I learned at the Savoy in London when I worked there and it was always part of the bread basket offered at lunch and dinner.

35 g/⅓ cup chopped pecans

35 g/⅓ cup sultanas/golen raisins

200 g/1⅔ cups white strong/bread flour

50 g/⅓ cup wholemeal/whole-wheat flour

5 g/1 teaspoon salt

3 g fresh yeast or 2 g/¾ teaspoon dried/active dry yeast

180 g/180 ml/¾ cup warm water

baking sheet lined with parchment paper

MAKES 1 SMALL LOAF

1 Mix the pecans and sultanas/golden raisins and set aside.

2 In one (smaller) mixing bowl, mix the flour and salt together and set aside. This is the dry mixture.

3 In another (larger) mixing bowl, weigh out the yeast. Add the water and stir until the yeast has dissolved. This is the wet mixture.

4 Add the dry mixture to the wet mixture.

5 Mix the mixtures together with a wooden spoon and then your hands until they come together to form a dough.

6 Cover with the bowl that had the dry mixture in it.

7 Let stand for 10 minutes.

8 After 10 minutes, add the pecan mixture to the dough. Knead gently as in Step 10 on page 20, taking care not to squash the sultanas/golden raisins.

9 Cover the bowl again and let stand for 10 minutes.

10 Repeat Steps 8 and 9 twice, then Step 8 again. Cover the bowl again and let rise for 1 hour.

11 When the dough has doubled in volume, punch it down with your fist to release the air.

12 Lightly dust a clean work surface with flour. Transfer the ball of dough to the floured work surface.

13 Fold one edge of the dough over into the middle. Fold the opposite edge over to the middle. **(A) (B)**

14 Now roll the dough to make a sausage. Make the ends tapered. **(C)**

15 Sprinkle flour over the bread. Score diagonal lines along the surface using a sharp, serrated knife. **(D)**

16 Place on the prepared baking sheet. Cover and let rise until slightly less than double the size – about 30–45 minutes.

17 About 20 minutes before baking, preheat the oven to 240°C (475°F) Gas 9. Place a roasting pan at the bottom of the oven to preheat. Fill a cup with water and set aside.

18 When the dough has finished rising, remove the bowl or covering.

19 Place the bread in the preheated oven, pour the reserved cupful of water onto the hot roasting pan and lower the oven temperature to 200°C (400°F) Gas 6.

20 Bake for about 30 minutes, or until golden brown.

21 To check if it is baked through, tip it upside down and tap the bottom – it should sound hollow.

22 If it is not ready, return to the oven for a few minutes. If it is ready, set it on a wire rack to cool.

A   B   C   D

BEER BREAD

The beer I have used in this bread is nettle ale, although any beer is worth trying. The beer is used instead of water and gives a wonderful extra dimension to the loaf. This is a great bread to make cheese and chutney sandwiches with.

A

B

C

D

E

400 g/3¼ cups malthouse flour
(or 2 cups unbleached bread flour,
¾ cup multigrain blend or medium rye
flour and ½ malted wheat flakes)

10 g/1 teaspoon salt

200 g/1⅔ cups malthouse or
unbleached strong/bread flour

2 g fresh yeast or 1 g/¼ teaspoon
dried/active dry yeast

200 g/200 ml/6 oz. organic ale or
other beer

4 g fresh yeast or 2 g/¾ teaspoon
dried/active dry yeast

200 g/200 ml/6 oz. organic ale or
other beer

rolled oats, for coating

*long proofing/dough-rising basket
(900-g/2-lb. capacity), greased*
baking sheet lined with parchment paper

MAKES 4 ROLLS

1 Into one (medium) mixing bowl, sift
the 400 g/3¼ cups malthouse flour (or
equivalent) and empty the sifted larger
grains into a shallow dish. Set aside.

2 Mix the salt with the sifted flour and set
aside. This is the dry mixture.

3 Into another (smaller) mixing bowl, sift
the 200 g/1⅔ cups malthouse flour and
empty the sifted larger grains into the dish
with the rest of the reserved grains.

4 In another (larger) mixing bowl, weigh
out the 2 g fresh yeast or equivalent. Add

the 200 g/200 ml/6 oz. ale and stir until
the yeast has dissolved. This is the wet
mixture. (Leave the second batch of ale in
a cool place, but not in the refrigerator.) **(A)**

5 Mix the 200 g/1⅔ cups sifted flour into
the wet mixture until it comes together.
(B) (C)

6 Cover and let ferment overnight in a
cool place.

7 The next day, in a (smaller) mixing bowl,
weigh out the 4 g fresh yeast or equivalent.
Add the remaining 200 g/200 ml/6 oz. ale

and stir until the yeast has dissolved.
(Don't worry if the ale has gone flat.) Pour
into the fermented ale mixture and mix.

8 Now add the reserved dry mixture and
mix with a wooden spoon until it comes
together. **(D) (E)**

9 Cover with the bowl that had the dry
mixture in it and let stand for 10 minutes.

10 After 10 minutes, knead as in Step 10
on page 20. Cover the bowl again and let
stand for 10 minutes.

11 Repeat Step 10 three times, but the last rising should be for 1 hour. **(F)**

12 When the dough has doubled in volume, punch it down. Lightly dust a clean work surface with flour. Transfer the ball of dough to the floured work surface.

13 Divide the dough into 4 equal portions using a metal dough scraper or sharp, serrated knife. **(G)**

14 Take each portion of dough and roll between your hands until you get a perfectly round, smooth ball. **(H)**

15 Add as many oats as you like to the reserved dish of malted grains and mix.

16 Roll the top of each ball of dough in the grain mixture. Place, grain-side down, in the prepared proofing basket. **(I)**

17 Let the dough rise until slightly less than double the size – 30–45 minutes. **(J)**

18 About 20 minutes before baking, preheat the oven to 240°C (475°F) Gas 9 and put a baking stone in to heat up. Place a roasting pan at the bottom of the oven to preheat. Fill a cup with water.

19 Tip the basket upside down onto the bread peel and lift it away from the risen dough. Slide the bread onto the hot baking stone, pour the reserved cupful of water onto the hot roasting pan and lower the oven temperature to 200°C (400°F) Gas 6. **(K)**

20 Bake for 30 minutes, or until golden.

21 To check if it is baked through, tip it upside down and tap the bottom – it should sound hollow.

22 If it is not ready, return to the oven for a few minutes. Set it on a wire rack to cool.

A B C D
E F G H

BAGUETTES MADE WITH A POOLISH

This is the traditional way of making baguettes, using the 'poolish' (pre-ferment) method whereby a wet sponge is left to ferment overnight before adding the rest of the ingredients. It is well worth the time and effort for the authentic flavour it produces.

2 g fresh yeast or 1 g/
¼ teaspoon dried/active
dry yeast

125 g/125 ml/½ cup warm water

125 g/1 cup white/unbleached
plain/all-purpose flour or French
T55 flour

300 g/2⅓ cups white/
unbleached plain/all-purpose
flour or French T55 flour

5 g/1 teaspoon salt

2 g fresh yeast or 1 g/
¼ teaspoon dried/active
dry yeast

140 g/140 ml/½ cup plus
1 tablespoon warm water

proofing linen or clean tea/
kitchen towel

baking sheet

floured long baguette bread
peel (optional)

parchment paper

MAKES 3 BAGUETTES

1 In a (larger) mixing bowl, weigh out the 2 g fresh yeast or equivalent. Add the 125 g/125 ml/½ cup water and stir until the yeast has dissolved. Add the 125 g/1 cup flour and mix with a wooden spoon until a smooth paste forms. Cover the bowl and let ferment overnight at room temperature. This is the poolish.

2 The next day, in a (smaller) mixing bowl, mix the 300 g/2⅓ cups flour and the salt together and set aside. This is the dry mixture.

3 In another (smaller) mixing bowl, weigh out the remaining 2 g fresh yeast or equivalent. Add the 140 g/140 ml/½ cup plus 1 tablespoon water and stir until the yeast has dissolved.

4 Mix the yeast solution into the poolish, then add the dry mixture too and mix with your hands until it comes together. **(A) (B)**

5 Cover and let stand for 10 minutes.

6 After 10 minutes, knead as in Step 10 on page 20.

7 Cover the bowl again and let stand for 10 minutes.

8 Repeat Steps 6 and 7 twice, then Step 6 again. **(C)**

9 Cover the bowl again and let rise for 1 hour.

10 Lightly dust a clean work surface with flour. Punch down the dough and transfer to the floured surface. Divide into 3 equal portions – weigh each piece and add or subtract dough until they all weigh the same. **(D)**

11 Gently flatten each ball of dough into an oval. Pull both ends of the oval out, then fold them over into the middle. You will now have a roughly rectangular shape. **(E) (F)**

12 Pull and fold the top of the rectangle one third of the way toward the middle, pressing it into the dough. Swivel it 180° and repeat. Repeat until you have a neat, long loaf shape. **(G) (H)**

13 Repeat with the remaining portions of dough. Cover the loaves (seam-side down) and let rest for 15 minutes. **(I)**

14 Turn one loaf over and flatten slightly. Fold the top right of the rectangle one third of the way toward the middle, pressing it into the dough. Repeat with the top left and repeat until rolled up. **(J) (K)**

15 Roll the dough between your hands until you get a baguette about the length of your baking sheet or the desired length. Repeat with the remaining dough. **(L)**

16 Dust the proofing linen with flour and lay it on the baking sheet. Arrange the baguettes on the cloth, seam-side up, pulling a bit of excess cloth between each baguette to separate them. **(M)**

17 Cover with the cloth and let rise until double the size – about 1 hour. **(N)**

18 About 20 minutes before baking, preheat the oven to 240°C (475°F) Gas 9. Place a roasting pan at the bottom of the oven to preheat. Fill a cup with water and set aside.

19 When the dough has finished rising, turn the baguettes over with a peel, if using, onto a paper-lined baking sheet. Dust them with flour and slash along their lengths using a lamé or serrated knife. **(O) (P: shows the baguettes on a peel before baking)**

20 Put in the preheated oven and pour the reserved cupful of water onto the hot roasting pan.

21 Bake for about 10–15 minutes, or until golden brown. To check if baked through, tip one upside down and tap the bottom – it should sound hollow. If ready, set it on a wire rack to cool.

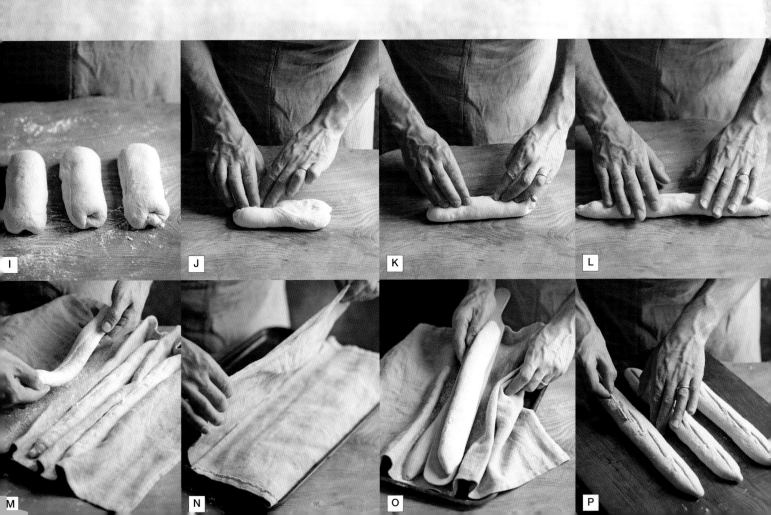

TSOUREKI

Tsoureki is a beautiful sweet bread used to break the fast at Eastertime in Greece. I always remember making lots and lots of these breads when I worked in Greece, together with the red, dyed eggs that are often placed in the middle of the tsoureki. I also have fond memories of this bread from my childhood.

40 g fresh yeast or 20 g/2 tablespoons dried/active dry yeast

50 g/50 ml/¼ cup warm water

40 g/⅓ cup white strong/bread flour

30 g/2 tablespoons unsalted butter (plus a pinch of salt) or salted butter

80 g/⅓ cup sugar

grated zest of ½ orange

4 g/1 teaspoon ground mahlepi/mahleb (ground black cherry pits)

4 g/1 teaspoon ground cardamom

1 medium egg

200 g/1⅔ cups white strong/bread flour

1 medium egg, beaten with a pinch of salt, for the egg wash

baking sheet lined with parchment paper or 500-g/6 x 4-in. loaf pan, greased with vegetable oil

MAKES 1 SMALL LOAF

1 In a (larger) mixing bowl, weigh out the 40 g fresh yeast or equivalent. Add the water and stir until the yeast has dissolved. Add the 40 g/⅓ cup flour and mix with a wooden spoon until well mixed. This is the pre-ferment.

2 Cover the bowl and let the mixture ferment in a cool place until doubled in size – about 30 minutes.

3 While the pre-ferment rises, melt the butter in a saucepan.

4 Add the sugar to the melted butter and turn down the heat to low. Stir with a wooden spoon.

5 When the sugar has dissolved, take the pan off the heat and mix in the orange zest and spices. Let cool, whisking from time to time.

6 Whisk the egg into the warm butter mixture until thoroughly combined.

7 When the pre-ferment is ready, uncover – it should look spongy. Add the 200 g/1⅔ cups flour and butter mixture and mix until it comes together. It will be quite stiff.

8 Cover and let stand for 10 minutes.

9 After 10 minutes, knead as in Step 10 on page 20.

10 Cover the bowl again and let stand for 10 minutes.

11 Repeat Steps 9 and 10 twice, then Step 9 again.

12 Cover the bowl and let rise for 1 hour.

13 When the dough has doubled in volume, punch down with your fist.

14 Lightly dust a clean work surface with flour. Transfer the dough to the floured surface and divide into 4 equal portions – weigh each piece and add or subtract dough until they all weigh the same.

15 Roll out each piece into a sausage about 25 cm/10 inches long, tapered at the end. Lay them out on the work surface, side by side, in a 'V' shape and press the ends together at the base of the 'V' to seal. Now refer to the step-by-step pictures on the following page to plait/braid the lengths of dough into a tsoureki shape.

16 Make sure the ends of the tsoureki are neatly tucked in. Place on the prepared baking sheet or snugly inside the prepared loaf pan.

17 Cover and let rise until slightly less than double the size – about 30–45 minutes.

18 About 20 minutes before baking, preheat the oven to 240°C (475°F) Gas 9. Place a roasting pan at the bottom of the oven to preheat. Fill a cup with water and set aside.

19 When the tsoureki has finished rising, brush it all over with the egg wash.

20 Place the tsoureki in the preheated oven, pour the reserved cupful of water onto the hot roasting pan and lower the oven temperature to 200°C (400°F) Gas 6.

21 Bake for about 20 minutes, or until golden brown.

22 To check if it is baked through, tip it upside down and tap the bottom – it should sound hollow. If it is ready, set it on a wire rack to cool.

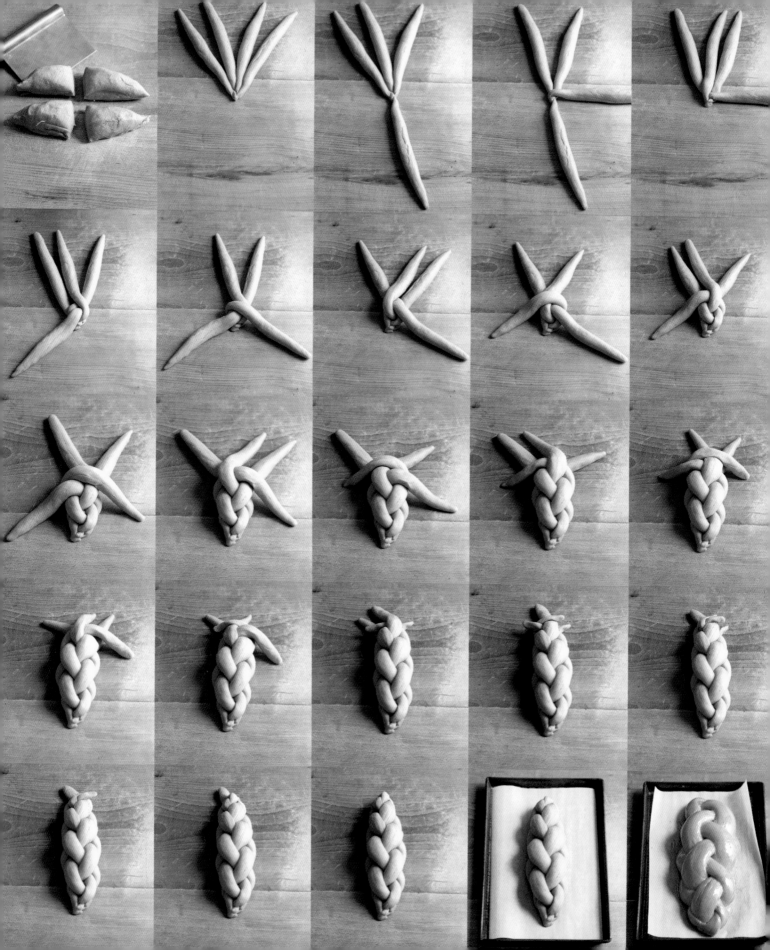

CHALLAH

Challah is the Jewish sabbath bread and it can be made in a simple spiral shape, as described here, or plaited/braided with 4 or 6 strands (shown opposite). Challah has a very delicate taste and can be eaten with either savoury or sweet food.

250 g/2 cups white strong/bread flour

4 g/¾ teaspoon salt

15 g/1 tablespoon sugar

6 g fresh yeast or 3 g/1 teaspoon dried/active dry yeast

80 g/80 ml/⅓ cup warm water

1 medium egg yolk

1 whole medium egg

20 g/20 ml/1 generous tablespoon sunflower oil

1 medium egg, beaten with a pinch of salt, for the egg wash

poppy or sesame seeds

baking sheet lined with parchment paper

MAKES 1 SMALL LOAF

1 In one (smaller) mixing bowl, mix the flour, salt and sugar together and set aside. This is the dry mixture.

2 In a (larger) mixing bowl, weigh out the yeast. Add the water and stir until the yeast has dissolved.

3 Lightly beat together the egg yolk and whole egg, then add to the yeast solution. This is the wet mixture.

4 Add the dry mixture to the wet mixture.

5 Mix the mixtures together with a wooden spoon and then mix in the oil until well combined.

6 Cover with the bowl that had the dry mixture in it.

7 Cover and let stand for 10 minutes.

8 After 10 minutes, knead as in Step 10 on page 20.

9 Cover the bowl again and let stand for 10 minutes.

10 Repeat Steps 8 and 9 twice, then Step 8 again.

11 Cover the bowl and let rise for 1 hour.

12 When the dough has doubled in volume, punch it down with your fist to release the air.

13 Lightly dust a clean work surface with flour. Remove the ball of dough from the bowl and place it on the floured work surface.

14 Roll it with your hands until you have one long sausage of dough with tapered ends. (Alternatively, at this stage you can divide the dough into 6 or 4 equal portions, roll into long sausages and plait/braid in the traditional way.)

15 Roll up the length of dough into a tight snail shape, tucking in the ends. Place on the prepared baking sheet. **(A)**

16 Brush it all over with the egg wash. **(B)**

17 Sprinkle with poppy or sesame seeds. **(C)**

18 Cover and let rise until slightly less than double the size – about 30–45 minutes. **(D)**

19 About 20 minutes before baking, preheat the oven to 240°C (475°F) Gas 9. Place a roasting pan at the bottom of the oven to preheat. Fill a cup with water and set aside.

20 Place the challah in the preheated oven, pour the reserved cupful of water onto the hot roasting pan and lower the oven temperature to 200°C (400°F) Gas 6.

21 Bake for about 20 minutes, or until golden brown.

22 To check if it is baked through, tip it upside down and tap the bottom – it should sound hollow.

23 If it is not ready, return to the oven for a few minutes. If it is ready, set it on a wire rack to cool.

A

B

C

D

BAGELS

Traditionally filled with cream cheese and lox (smoked salmon), bagels now come in all sorts of flavours, both savoury and sweet. The boiling element of the baking process makes them an unusual type of bread, but it's this that makes them so deliciously chewy.

A

B

C

D

500 g/4 cups white strong/
bread flour

10 g/2 teaspoons salt

20 g/4 teaspoons sugar

25 g/2 tablespoons unsalted
or salted butter, softened and
finely chopped

5 g fresh or 3 g/1 teaspoon
dried/active dry yeast

240 g/240 ml/1 cup warm water

1 medium egg, lightly beaten

5 g/1 teaspoon salt

1 medium egg, beaten with a
pinch of salt, for the egg wash

poppy or sesame seeds
(optional)

*baking sheet lined with
parchment paper*

*1 saucepan, 2-litre/2-quart
capacity*

MAKES 9 BAGELS

1 In one (smaller) mixing bowl, mix the flour, 10 g/2 teaspoons salt, the sugar and butter together and set aside. This is the dry mixture.

2 In a (larger) mixing bowl, weigh out the yeast. Add the water to the bowl and stir until the yeast has dissolved.

3 Add the egg to the yeast solution and mix. This is the wet mixture.

4 Add the dry mixture to the wet mixture.

5 Mix the mixtures together with a wooden spoon until it comes together.

6 Cover with the bowl that had the dry mixture in it and let stand for 10 minutes.

7 After 10 minutes, knead as in Step 10 on page 20.

8 Cover the bowl again and let stand for 10 minutes.

9 Repeat Steps 7 and 8 twice and then Step 7 again.

10 Cover the bowl and let rise for 1 hour.

11 When the dough has doubled in volume, punch it down with your fist to release the air.

12 Lightly dust a clean work surface with flour. Remove the ball of dough from the bowl and place it on the floured work surface.

13 Roll the dough into a log, then cut into 9 equal portions using a metal dough scraper or sharp, serrated knife. Roll each into a ball.

14 Take each ball of dough and push your finger through the middle..Keep working to make a neat hole. **(A)**

15 Place the bagels on the prepared baking sheet, cover and let rest for 10 minutes. **(B)**

16 Just before the bagel dough has finished resting, half-fill the 2-litre/2-quart saucepan with water, add the 5 g/1 teaspoon salt and bring to the boil.

17 Cook the bagels in batches of 3 or 4 in the boiling water until they rise up.

18 Turn the bagels over and boil for a further 5 minutes. **(C)**

19 Transfer the boiled bagels to the baking sheet again and let cool slightly.

20 Preheat the oven to 240°C (475°F) Gas 9. Place a roasting pan at the bottom of the oven to preheat. Fill a cup with water and set aside.

21 Brush the egg wash over the bagels.

22 For seeded bagels, dip the egg-washed bagels in poppy or sesame seeds and return to the baking sheet. **(D)**

23 Place the bagels in the preheated oven, pour the reserved cupful of water onto the hot roasting pan and lower the oven temperature to 200°C (400°F) Gas 6.

24 Bake the bagels for about 15 minutes, or until golden brown.

25 To check if they are baked through, tip one upside down and tap the bottom – it should sound hollow.

26 If they are not ready, return to the oven for a few minutes. If they are ready, set them on a wire rack to cool.

A   B   C   D   E   F

PITA BREADS

Pita breads are quite exciting to watch in the oven – they puff up in no time – and make perfect pockets for stuffing with all sorts of delicious fillings.

200 g/1⅔ cups plain/all-purpose flour

4 g/¾ teaspoon salt

2 g fresh or 1 g/¼ teaspoon dried/active dry yeast

120 g/120 ml/½ cup warm water

roasting pan

MAKES 6 MINI PITA BREADS

1 In one (smaller) mixing bowl, mix the flour and salt together and set aside. This is the dry mixture.

2 In another (larger) mixing bowl, weigh out the yeast. Add the water and stir until the yeast has dissolved. This is the wet mixture.

3 Add the dry mixture to the wet mixture.

4 Mix the mixtures together with a wooden spoon and then your hands until they come together to form a dough.

5 Cover with the bowl that had the dry mixture in it and let stand for 10 minutes.

6 After 10 minutes, knead gently as in Step 10 on page 20.

7 Cover the bowl again and let stand for 10 minutes.

8 Repeat Steps 6 and 7 twice, then Step 6 again. **(A)**

9 Cover the bowl again and let rise for 1 hour.

10 When the dough has doubled in volume, punch it down with your fist to release the air.

11 Lightly dust a clean work surface with flour. Remove the ball of dough from the bowl and place it on the floured work surface.

12 Divide the dough into 6 equal portions using a metal dough scraper or sharp, serrated knife. If you want to be as accurate as possible, weigh each piece and add or subtract dough from the portions until they all weigh the same. **(B)**

13 Take one portion of dough and roll between your hands to make a ball. Repeat with the remaining dough. **(C)**

14 Cover and let rest for 10 minutes.

15 Preheat the oven to 240°C (475°F) Gas 9 and place a roasting pan on the middle rack to preheat.

16 Using a rolling pin, roll out each ball. Cover and let rise for 10 minutes. **(D) (E)**

17 When the dough has finished rising, dust the pita breads with flour and place on the preheated roasting pan in the oven.

18 Bake until completely puffed up. The time will vary, so keep an eye on them. Don't worry if they are no longer round when baked – the important thing is that they puff up! **(F)**

19 Set the pita breads to cool slightly on a wire rack, then place them, warm, in a food bag so that they don't dry out.

A

B

C

D

ARMENIAN FLATBREADS

This delicate, crisp flatbread was another item in the bread basket at the Savoy when I worked there. It's perfect with a glass of wine as a snack or apéritif.

30 g/30 ml/
2 tablespoons olive oil

30 g/30 ml/
2 tablespoons water

1 garlic clove, crushed

160 g/1¼ cups white
strong/bread flour

5 g/1 teaspoon salt

50 g/50 ml/
3 tablespoons olive oil

75 g/75 ml/⅓ cup water

½ onion, thinly sliced

FOR SPRINKLING

poppyseeds

nigella seeds (black
onion seeds)

sesame seeds

*4 baking sheets lined
with parchment paper*

**MAKES ABOUT 24
FLATBREADS**

1 Put the 30 g/30 ml/2 tablespoons olive oil, 30 g/30 ml/2 tablespoons water and garlic in a small bowl and let infuse.

2 In one (smaller) mixing bowl, mix the flour and salt together and set aside. This is the dry mixture.

3 In another (smaller) mixing bowl, mix the 50 g/50 ml/3 tablespoons olive oil and the 75 g/75 ml/⅓ cup water. Add the dry mixture and mix until it comes together.

4 Cover with the bowl that had the dry mixture in it.

5 Let stand for 5 minutes.

6 After 5 minutes, knead gently as in Step 10 on page 20.

7 Cover the bowl again and let stand for 5 minutes.

8 Repeat Steps 6 and 7 twice, then Step 6 again. The dough should be smooth and elastic.

9 Cover the bowl again and let rise for 30 minutes.

10 After 30 minutes, divide the dough into 4 roughly equal portions using a metal dough scraper or sharp, serrated knife.

11 Lay out your 4 prepared baking sheets.

12 Put one portion of dough in the middle of one baking sheet. Press on it with your hand to flatten slightly, then start to pull the corners of the dough outward. **(A) (B)**

13 Keep pulling and stretching from each corner until you get a very thin, rough rectangle about the size of the baking sheet. **(C) (D)**

14 Let rest for 15 minutes and preheat the oven to 180°C (350°F) Gas 4.

15 While it is resting, work on the second portion of dough on another baking sheet. If you find that the dough is breaking, stop and let it rest for a few minutes while you work on another portion of dough.

16 When all the dough has rested, brush the infused garlic oil all over the flatbreads. **(E)**

17 Cut each flatbread into 6 using a sharp knife. **(F)**

18 Sprinkle the sliced onion and the seeds evenly over all the flatbreads.

19 Bake the flatbreads in the preheated oven in batches for 5–10 minutes, or until golden brown.

20 Let cool on wire racks.

WHEAT-FREE
OR GLUTEN-FREE
BREADS

DARK RYE BREAD

I learned my trade as a baker in a German-style bakery. There, rye bread was always made in large quantities, as it was so popular with our customers due to its quality and taste. This is 100% dark rye bread and it's one of my all-time favourites.

150 g/1¼ cups dark rye/pumpernickel flour
100 g/scant ½ cup rye sourdough starter (see page 11)
200 g/200 ml/¾ cup plus 1 tablespoon cold water
200 g/1⅓ cups dark rye/pumpernickel flour
6 g/1 teaspoon salt
150 g/150 ml/⅔ cup hot water

500-g/6 x 4-in. loaf pan, greased with vegetable oil

MAKES 1 MEDIUM LOAF

1 In one (larger) mixing bowl, mix the 150 g /1¼ cups flour, sourdough starter and 200 g /200 ml/¾ cup plus 1 tablespoon cold water until well combined. Place a smaller mixing bowl upside down over it and let ferment overnight. This is the wet mixture.

2 The next day, in another mixing bowl, mix the 200 g/1⅓ cups flour and salt together. This is the dry mixture.

3 Tip the dry mixture over the wet mixture, making sure you entirely cover the wet mixture with the dry. Do not mix yet. **(A)**

A

B

C

D

E

F

4 Carefully pour the 150 g/150 ml/⅔ cup hot water over the dry mixture. **(B)**

5 Quickly mix together with a wooden spoon – you don't want the hot water to have time to react with the flour. **(C)**

6 Spoon the mixture into the prepared loaf pan. **(D)**

7 Dip a plastic scraper or tablespoon in water and use to smooth the surface of the dough. **(E)**

8 Dust the loaf with flour. **(F)**

9 Cover the loaf and let rise for 2 hours.

10 The bread will rise now and when it is baked, but not all that much, which is why we are using such a small loaf pan for a relatively large quantity of dough. **(G)**

11 About 15 minutes before baking, preheat the oven to 240°C (475°F) Gas 9. Place a roasting pan at the bottom of the oven to preheat. Fill a cup with water and set aside.

12 When the dough has finished rising, remove the bowl or covering.

13 Place the loaf in the preheated oven, pour the reserved cupful of water onto the hot roasting pan and lower the oven temperature to 220°C (425°F) Gas 7.

14 Bake the bread for about 30 minutes, or until brown.

15 Turn the bread out of the loaf pan and set on a wire rack to cool. **(H)**

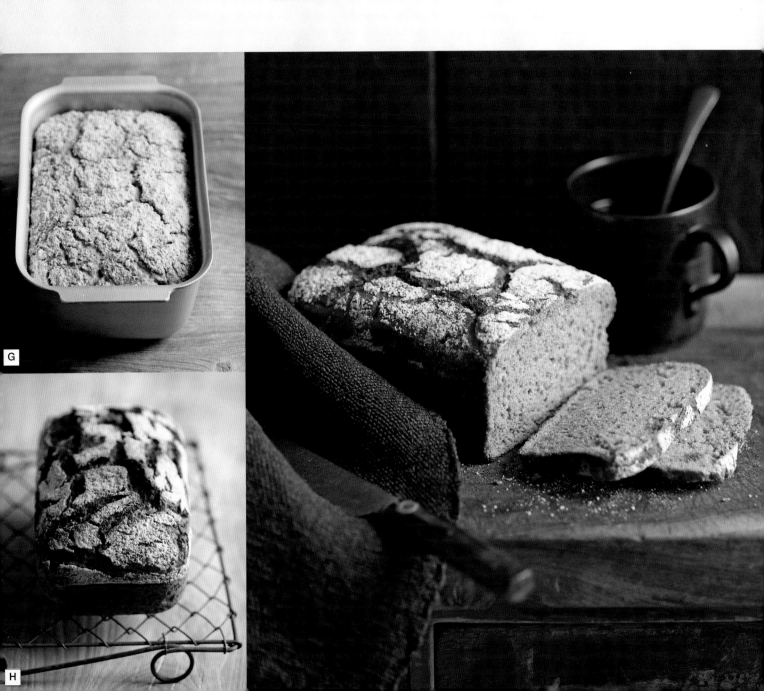

PRUNE AND PEPPER RYE BREAD

You might wonder why I would put prune and pepper together in a bread. Wait until you taste it! The sweetness of the prunes together with the sourness of the rye and the hit of spicy peppercorns really works. It is delicious!

150 g/1¼ cups dark rye/pumpernickel flour

100 g/scant ½ cup rye sourdough starter (see page 11)

200 g/200 ml/¾ cup plus 1 tablespoon cold water

200 g/1⅓ cups dark rye/pumpernickel flour

6 g/1 teaspoon salt

150 g/150 ml/⅔ cup hot water

200 g/1¼ cups chopped pitted prunes

½–1 tablespoon whole pink peppercorns

900-g/8½ x 4½-in. loaf pan, greased with vegetable oil

MAKES 1 LARGE LOAF

1 In one (larger) mixing bowl, mix the 150 g /1¼ cups flour, the sourdough starter and the 200 g/200 ml/¾ cup plus 1 tablespoon cold water until well combined. This is the wet mixture. **(A)**

2 Place a smaller mixing bowl upside down over the wet mixture to cover and let ferment overnight.

3 The next day, in another mixing bowl, mix the 200 g/1⅓ cups flour and salt together. This is the dry mixture.

4 Tip the dry mixture over the wet mixture, making sure you entirely cover the wet mixture with the dry. Do not mix yet. **(B)**

5 Carefully pour the 150 g/150 ml/⅔ cup hot water over the dry mixture.

6 Quickly mix together with a wooden spoon – you don't want the hot water to have time to react with the flour. **(C)**

7 Tip the prunes and peppercorns (between ½ and 1 tablespoon depending on your preference) into the mixture. **(D)**

8 Mix with a wooden spoon until well combined. **(E)**

9 Now continue following the method for the Dark Rye Bread from Step 6 on page 71. (You can omit the step for dusting the loaf with flour if you like.)

RAISIN RYE BREAD

This bread is very fruity, so partners beautifully with cheese. I always opt for sultanas (golden raisins) over raisins and currants for their sweetness. We were fortunate to get a Great Taste Award for a version of this bread at Judges Bakery in Hastings.

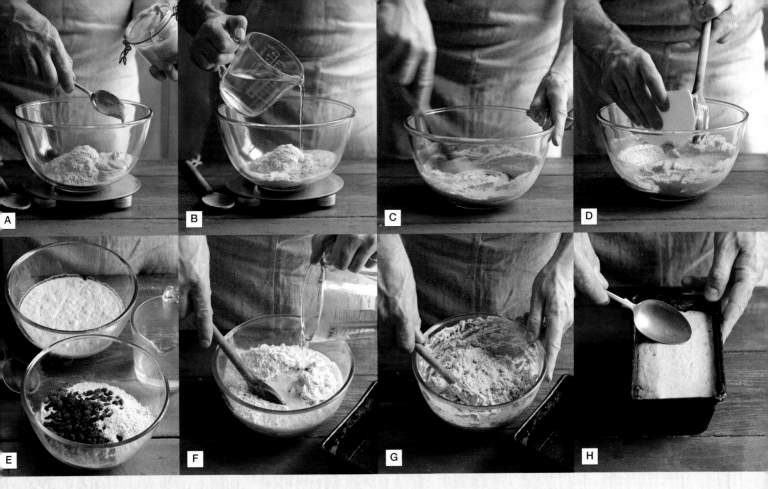

150 g/1¼ cups dark rye/
pumpernickel flour

100 g/scant ½ cup rye
sourdough starter (see
page 11)

200 g/200 ml/¾ cup
plus 1 tablespoon
cold water

200 g/1⅓ cups dark rye/
pumpernickel flour

6 g/1 teaspoon salt

200 g/1¾ cups sultanas/
golden raisins

150 g/150 ml/⅔ cup
hot water

900-g/8½ x 4½-in. loaf
pan, greased with
vegetable oil

MAKES 1 LARGE LOAF

1 In one (larger) mixing bowl, mix the 150 g/
1¼ cups flour, the sourdough starter and the
200 g/200 ml/¾ cup plus 1 tablespoon cold water
until well combined. Use a plastic scraper or spatula
to scrape the mixture off the spoon and around the
edge of the bowl. Place a smaller mixing bowl upside
down over it to cover and let ferment overnight. This
is the wet mixture. **(A) (B) (C) (D)**

2 The next day, in another mixing bowl, mix the
200 g/1⅓ cups flour, salt and sultanas/golden raisins
together. This is the dry mixture. **(E)**

3 Tip the dry mixture over the wet mixture, making
sure you entirely cover the wet mixture with the dry.
Do not mix yet.

4 Carefully pour the 150 g/150 ml/⅔ cup hot water
over the dry mixture. **(F)**

5 Quickly mix together with a wooden spoon – you
don't want the hot water to have time to react with
the flour. **(G)**

6 Spoon the mixture into the prepared loaf pan.

7 Dip a plastic scraper or tablespoon in water and
use to smooth the surface of the dough. **(H)**

8 Cover the loaf and let rise for 2 hours.

9 About 15 minutes before baking, preheat the oven
to 240°C (475°F) Gas 9. Place a roasting pan at the
bottom of the oven to preheat. Fill a cup with water
and set aside.

10 When the dough has finished rising, remove the
bowl or covering.

11 Place the loaf in the preheated oven, pour the
reserved cupful of water onto the hot roasting pan
and lower the oven temperature to 220°C (425°F)
Gas 7.

12 Bake for about 30 minutes, or until brown.

13 Turn the bread out of the loaf pan and set on a
wire rack to cool.

A   B   C   D

WHOLEGRAIN RYE BREAD

Wholegrain rye bread is my version of pumpernickel and you will either love it or hate it. You can make it with chopped/cracked rye or wheat. Either way, you have to be very patient because it needs to ferment overnight and then rest for up to 8 hours. In Namibia where I qualified as a confectioner and baker, we made lots of this kind of bread. True pumpernickel is baked for 18 hours at 100°C/212°F to produce that distinct malty flavour.

350 g/2⅓ cups chopped/cracked rye (or chopped/cracked wheat)

6 g/1 teaspoon salt

100 g/a scant ½ cup rye sourdough starter (see page 11)

350 g/350 ml/1½ cups warm water

500-g/6 x 4-in. loaf pan, greased with vegetable oil

MAKES 1 LARGE LOAF

1 In one (smaller) mixing bowl, mix the chopped/cracked rye or wheat and the salt together. This is the dry mixture.

2 In another (larger) mixing bowl, mix the sourdough starter and water together until well combined. This is the wet mixture.

3 Add the dry mixture to the wet mixture and mix until thoroughly combined. **(A: wheat) (B: rye)**

4 Cover with the bowl that had the dry mixture in it.

5 Let ferment in a cool place overnight.

6 The next day, spoon the mixture into the prepared loaf pan.

7 Dip a plastic scraper or tablespoon in water and use to smooth the surface of the dough. **(C: wheat, left; rye, right)**

8 Cover the loaf pan and let rest for 6–8 hours.

9 The dough will not rise much, but you will notice little air holes forming on the surface. (Since the bread hardly rises, we only need a small loaf pan even for a relatively large quantity of dough.) **(D: wheat, left; rye, right)**

10 About 15 minutes before baking, preheat the oven to 240°C (475°F) Gas 9. Place a roasting pan at the bottom of the oven to preheat. Fill a cup with water and set aside.

11 When the dough has finished rising, remove the bowl or covering.

12 Place the loaf in the preheated oven, pour the reserved cupful of water onto the hot roasting pan and lower the temperature to 220°C (425°F) Gas 7.

13 Bake for about 30 minutes, or until brown.

14 Turn the bread out of the loaf pan and set on a wire rack to cool.

KAMUT OR SPELT BREAD

Kamut and spelt are known as ancient grains. They have become popular due to their taste and digestibility. For the time being, spelt flour is more widely available than Kamut, but Kamut is often sold in health food stores.

300 g/2½ cups Kamut (khorasan) flour or (wholegrain) spelt flour

6 g/1 teaspoon salt

3 g fresh yeast or 2 g/¾ teaspoon dried/active dry yeast

200–230 g/230 ml/up to 1 cup warm water

500-g/6 x 4-in. loaf pan, greased with vegetable oil

MAKES 1 SMALL LOAF

1 In one (smaller) mixing bowl, mix the flour and salt together and set aside. This is the dry mixture.

2 In another (larger) mixing bowl, weigh out the yeast. Add the water and stir until the yeast has dissolved. (You will need slightly less water if you are using Kamut flour.) This is the wet mixture.

3 Add the dry mixture to the wet mixture. Mix with a wooden spoon and then your hands until they come together to form a dough.

4 Cover with the bowl that had the dry mixture in it and let stand for 10 minutes.

5 Knead the dough as in Step 10 on page 20.

6 Cover the bowl again and let stand for 10 minutes.

7 Repeat Steps 5 and 6 twice, then Step 5 again. Cover the bowl again and let rise for 1 hour.

8 Punch down the dough with your fist.

9 Lightly dust a clean work surface with flour.

10 Remove the dough from the bowl and place on the floured work surface. **(A)**

11 Gently flatten into an oval. Fold the right end over into the middle, then the left. **(B) (C)**

12 Press down slightly to seal the dough together. You will now have a roughly rectangular shape. Pull and fold the top of the rectangle one third of the way toward the middle, pressing it into the dough.

13 Swivel it 180° and keep folding as in Step 12 until you have a shape roughly the size of your loaf pan. **(D) (E) (F)**

14 Place the dough inside the prepared loaf pan, seam-side down. **(G: Kamut, left; spelt, right)**

15 Cover the loaf pan and let rise until slightly less than double the size – about 30–45 minutes.

16 About halfway through the rising, preheat the oven to 240°C (475°F) Gas 9. Place a roasting pan at the bottom of the oven to preheat. Fill a cup with water and set aside.

17 When the dough has finished rising, remove the bowl or covering. **(H)**

18 Place the bread in the preheated oven. Pour the reserved cupful of water onto the hot roasting pan and lower the temperature to 220°C (425°F) Gas 7.

19 Bake for about 35 minutes, or until brown. Turn the bread out of the loaf pan and set on a wire rack to cool.

A   B   C

GLUTEN-FREE BREAD
WITH TWO VARIATIONS

I believe everybody should be able to eat bread of some kind. There are many gluten-free flour blends available but I have made my own that works well. Gluten-free bread needs to rest, but doesn't require kneading because there is no gluten to be worked.

PLAIN

150 g/1 cup potato flour

150 g/1 cup brown rice flour

80 g/½ cup plus 1 tablespoon buckwheat flour

80 g/½ cup plus 1 tablespoon coarse cornmeal/maize flour

10 g/2 teaspoons salt

14 g fresh yeast or 7 g/2¼ teaspoons dried/active dry yeast

360 g/360 ml/1½ cups warm water

900-g/8½ x 4½-in. loaf pan, greased with vegetable oil

MAKES 1 LARGE LOAF

SEEDED

100 g/⅔ cup potato flour

100 g/⅔ cup brown rice flour

50 g/⅓ cup buckwheat flour

150 g/1 cup kasha (buckwheat flakes)

10 g/2 teaspoons salt

40 g/⅓ cup sunflower seeds

40 g/⅓ cup pumpkin seeds

40 g/¼ cup linseed/flaxseed

20 g/2 tablespoons sesame seeds

20 g/2 tablespoons poppyseeds

10 g fresh yeast or 5 g/1½ teaspoons dried/active dry yeast

400 g/400 ml/1⅔ cups warm water

10 g/1 scant tablespoon blackstrap or dark molasses

SPICED FRUIT

125 g/1 scant cup potato flour

125 g/1 scant cup brown rice flour

75 g/⅔ cup buckwheat flour

75 g/½ cup plus 1 tablespoon coarse cornmeal/maize flour

10 g/2 teaspoons salt

75 g/½ cup (Zante) currants

75 g/½ cup sultanas/golden raisins

grated zest of 1 orange

grated zest of 1 lemon

1 teaspoon ground cinnamon

1 teaspoon ground ginger

a pinch of ground cloves

10 g fresh yeast or 5 g/1½ teaspoons dried/active dry yeast

300 g/300 ml/1¼ cups warm water

2 teaspoons honey

1 In one (smaller) bowl, mix the flours and salt together. If making the Seeded or Spiced Fruit Bread, mix in the seeds, dried fruit, zest and/or spices at this stage, too. This is the dry mixture. **(A)**

2 In another (larger) mixing bowl, weigh out the yeast. Add the water and stir until the yeast has dissolved. If making the Seeded or Spiced Fruit Bread, mix in the molasses or honey at this stage, too. This is the wet mixture.

3 Add the dry mixture to the wet mixture. **(B)**

4 Mix with a wooden spoon. The mixture should have the consistency of soft yogurt. If not, add a little more water to the mixture. **(C) (D)**

5 Cover and let rest for 1 hour. **(E)**

6 Pour the mixture into the prepared loaf pan. **(F) (G)**

7 Cover and let rise for 20–30 minutes, or until the dough has risen by 1–2 cm/½–¾ inch. **(H)**

8 Preheat the oven to 240°C (475°F) Gas 9. Place a roasting pan at the bottom of the oven to preheat. Fill a cup with water and set aside.

9 When the dough has finished rising, remove the bowl or the covering.

10 Place the risen bread in the preheated oven. Pour the reserved cupful of water onto the hot roasting pan and lower the temperature to 220°C (425°F) Gas 7.

11 Bake for about 30 minutes, or until golden brown.

12 Turn the bread out of the loaf pan and set on a wire rack to cool.

A   B   C

GLUTEN-FREE CORNBREAD

My gluten-free cornbread is made with yeast, but contains no eggs, so it really is more like traditional bread than many cornbread recipes. It is great for dipping into stews and mopping up sauces.

200 g/1½ cups fine
cornmeal/maize flour

50 g/⅓ cup potato flour

5 g/1 teaspoon salt

5 g fresh yeast or 3 g/
1 teaspoon dried/active
dry yeast

200 g/200 ml/¾ cup
plus 1 tablespoon
warm water

50 g/½ cup cooked corn
kernels (fresh, frozen or
canned and drained)

*16-cm/6½-inch round
cake pan, well greased
with vegetable oil*

**MAKES 1 SMALL
BREAD**

1 In one (smaller) mixing bowl, mix the flours and salt together and set aside. This is the dry mixture.

2 In another (larger) mixing bowl, weigh out the yeast.   Add the water and stir until the yeast has dissolved. This is the wet mixture.

3 Add the dry mixture and the corn kernels to the wet mixture. Mix with a wooden spoon. The mixture should have the consistency of soft yogurt. If not, add a little more water to the mixture.

4 Cover and let rest for 1 hour. **(A)**

5 Pour the mixture into the prepared cake pan. **(B)**

6 Cover and let rise until it just reaches the top of the pan – 30–45 minutes. **(C)**

7 About halfway through the rising, preheat the oven to 240°C (475°F) Gas 9. Place a roasting pan at the bottom of the oven to preheat. Fill a cup with water and set aside.

8 When the dough has finished rising, remove the bowl or covering.

9 Place the risen bread in the preheated oven. Pour the reserved cupful of water onto the hot roasting pan and lower the temperature to 220°C (425°F) Gas 7.

10 Bake the cornbread for about 35 minutes, or until golden brown.

11 Let cool in the cake pan and eat warm or cold, cut into wedges.

SOURDOUGHS

A

B

C

D

E

F

G

H

I

WHITE SOURDOUGH

This is a basic sourdough using white flour. I have made it in a small size – this way it is just enough for a meal. Now that you know how to make your own sourdough starter, bake this fantastic bread on a regular basis.

250 g/2 cups white
strong/bread flour

4 g/¾ teaspoon salt

150 g/150 ml/⅔ cup
warm water

75 g/⅓ cup white
sourdough starter
(see page 11)

proofing/dough-rising
basket (500-g/1-lb.
capacity) or colander

proofing linen or clean
tea/kitchen towel

floured bread peel and
baking stone (optional)

baking sheet lined with
parchment paper

MAKES 1 SMALL LOAF

1 In one (smaller) mixing bowl, mix the flour and salt together. This is the dry mixture. **(A)**

2 In another (larger) mixing bowl, weigh out the water and the sourdough starter. Stir until well combined. This is the wet mixture. **(B) (C)**

3 Add the dry mixture to the wet mixture. Mix together with a wooden spoon and then your hands until they come together to form a dough. Use a plastic scraper to scrape the side of the bowl clean and make sure all the ingredients are thoroughly mixed. **(D) (E) (F)**

4 Cover with the bowl that had the dry mixture in it and let stand for 10 minutes.

5 After 10 minutes, leaving the dough in the bowl, pull a portion of it up from the side and press it into the middle. Turn the bowl slightly and repeat this process with another portion of dough. Repeat another 8 times. The whole process should only take about 10 seconds and the dough should start to resist. **(G) (H)**

6 Cover the bowl again and let stand for 10 minutes.

7 Repeat Steps 5 and 6 twice, then Step 5 again. Cover the bowl and let rise for 1 hour. **(I)**

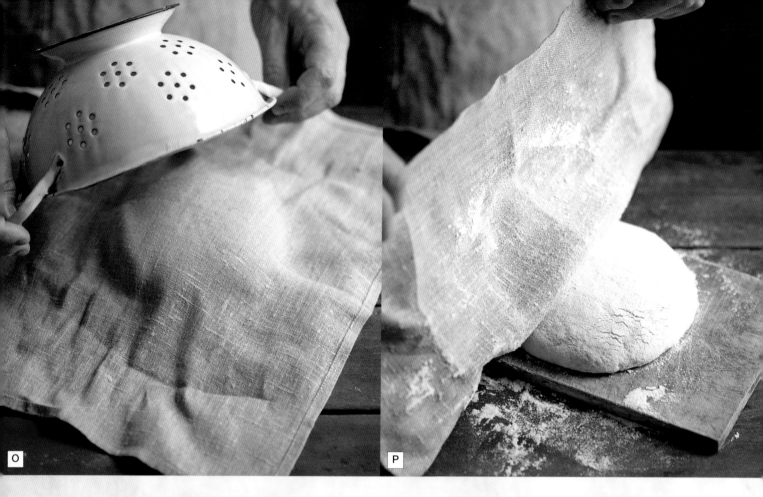

O

P

8 Lightly dust a clean work surface with flour. Put the dough on the work surface. **(J)**

9 Shape the dough into a smooth, rounded disc. **(K) (L)**

10 Line a proofing/dough-rising basket or a colander with proofing linen or a clean tea/kitchen towel. Dust liberally with flour and lay the dough inside it. **(M)**

11 Now dust the dough with flour. **(N)**

12 Let rise until about double the size – this will take between 3 and 6 hours.

13 About 20 minutes before baking, preheat the oven to 240°C (475°F) Gas 9. Place a roasting pan at the bottom of the oven to preheat. Fill a cup with water and set aside.

14 When the dough has doubled in volume, tip out of the basket or colander onto the bread peel or prepared baking sheet. **(O)**

15 Gently peel away the linen or towel. **(P)**

16 Take a pair of sharp kitchen scissors and snip cuts into the surface of the bread in a circular pattern. **(Q)**

17 Slide the bread into the preheated oven on its baking sheet, or if using a baking stone, slide it from the peel onto the hot stone. Pour the reserved cupful of water onto the hot roasting pan and lower the oven temperature to 220°C (425°F) Gas 7.

18 Bake for about 30 minutes, or until golden brown.

19 To check if the bread is baked through, tip it upside down and tap the bottom – it should sound hollow.

20 If it is not ready, return to the oven for a few minutes. If it is ready, set it on a wire rack to cool.

WHOLEGRAIN SOURDOUGH

This is just as simple a recipe as the White Sourdough on page 87, but to make it more wholesome, I have put in chopped/cracked wheat and wholemeal/whole-wheat flour to give it a nuttier flavour.

200 g/1⅓ cups chopped/cracked wheat

200 g/200 ml/1 scant cup warm water

400 g/3¼ cups wholemeal/whole-wheat flour

12 g/2 teaspoons salt

160 g/⅔ cup white or wholemeal/whole-wheat sourdough starter (see page 11)

at least 140 g/140 ml/⅔ cup warm water

wheatgerm and bran mixture, for coating (see Suppliers & Stockists, page 173)

long proofing/dough-rising basket (900-g/2-lb. capacity)

floured bread peel and baking stone (optional)

baking sheet lined with parchment paper

MAKES 1 LARGE LOAF

1 In one (smaller) mixing bowl, mix the chopped/cracked wheat and the 200 g/1 scant cup water and let soak until soft.

2 In another (smaller) bowl, mix the 400 g/3¼ cups flour and the salt together. This is the dry mixture.

3 In another (larger) mixing bowl, mix the sourdough starter and 140 g/140 ml/⅔ cup water together until well combined. Stir in the soaked wheat. This is the wet mixture.

4 Add the dry mixture to the wet mixture and mix until thoroughly combined. Add a little water if the dough is too stiff.

5 Cover with the bowl that had the dry mixture in it and let stand for 10 minutes.

6 After 10 minutes, knead the dough as in Step 5 on page 87.

7 Cover the bowl again and let stand for 10 minutes.

8 Repeat Steps 6 and 7 twice, then Step 6 again. Cover the bowl and let rise for 1 hour.

9 Lightly dust a clean work surface with the wheatgerm and bran mixture.

10 Put the dough on the work surface and roll with your hands, in the mixture, until roughly the length and width of your proofing basket. **(A)**

11 Sprinkle more of the wheatgerm and bran mixture inside the proofing basket and lay the bread inside it. **(B)**

12 Let the dough rise until about double the size – this will take between 3 and 6 hours. **(C)**

13 About 20 minutes before baking, preheat the oven to 240°C (475°F) Gas 9. Place a roasting pan at the bottom of the oven to preheat. Fill a cup with water and set aside.

14 When the dough has doubled in volume, tip it out of the basket onto the bread peel or prepared baking sheet. **(D)**

15 Slide the bread into the preheated oven on its baking sheet, or if using a baking stone, slide it from the peel onto the hot stone. Pour the reserved cupful of water onto the hot roasting pan and lower the oven temperature to 220°C (425°F) Gas 7.

16 Bake for about 30 minutes, or until brown.

17 To check if the bread is baked through, tip it upside down and tap the bottom – it should sound hollow.

18 If it is not ready, return to the oven for a few minutes. If it is ready, set it on a wire rack to cool.

A   B   C   D

'LEVAIN DE CAMPAGNE' BREAD

This is my version of a French-style sourdough, a 'country sourdough', which I created at Judges Bakery and for which I won a Great Taste Award.

250 g/2 cups white strong/bread flour

100 g/¾ cup wholemeal/whole-wheat flour

50 g/½ dark rye/pumpernickel flour

6 g/1 teaspoon salt

150 g/⅔ cup white sourdough starter (see page 11)

300 g/300 ml/1¼ cups warm water

round proofing/dough-rising basket (900-g/2-lb. capacity)

floured bread peel and baking stone (optional)

baking sheet lined with parchment paper

MAKES 1 LARGE LOAF

1 In one (smaller) mixing bowl, mix the flours and salt together. This is the dry mixture. **(A)**

2 In another (larger) mixing bowl, mix the sourdough starter and water together until well combined. This is the wet mixture. **(B)**

3 Add the dry mixture to the wet mixture and mix until it comes together. The mixture will be a bit soft, but don't despair and don't be tempted to add more flour! **(C) (D)**

4 Cover with the bowl that had the dry mixture in it and let stand for 10 minutes.

5 After 10 minutes, knead the dough as in Step 5 on page 87.

6 Cover the bowl again and let stand for 10 minutes.

7 Repeat Steps 5 and 6 twice, then Step 5 again.

8 Cover the bowl and let rise for 1 hour.

9 Lightly dust a clean work surface with flour. Put the dough on the work surface and shape into a smooth, rounded disc. **(E)**

10 Dust the proofing/dough-rising basket with flour. Lay the dough inside it and dust the dough with flour. **(F) (G)**

11 Let the dough rise until about double the size – this will take between 3 and 6 hours. **(H)**

12 About 20 minutes before baking, preheat the oven to 240°C (475°F) Gas 9. Place a roasting pan at the bottom of the oven to preheat. Fill a cup with water and set aside.

13 When the dough has doubled in volume, tip it out of the basket onto the bread peel or prepared baking sheet. **(I) (J)**

14 Slash a simple pattern on the surface of the bread using a sharp, serrated knife. **(K)**

15 Slide the bread into the preheated oven on its baking sheet, or if using a baking stone, slide it from the peel onto the hot stone. Pour the reserved cupful of water onto the hot roasting pan and lower the oven temperature to 220°C (425°F) Gas 7.

16 Bake for about 30 minutes, or until brown.

17 To check if the bread is baked through, tip it upside down and tap the bottom – it should sound hollow.

18 If it is not ready, return to the oven for a few minutes. If it is ready, set it on a wire rack to cool.

WHITE WHEY SOURDOUGH

You might ask why would I make a bread using whey. When I worked at Daylesford, we made cheddar on the premises, so I thought it would be exciting to make a sourdough using whey from the cheese making. I got a great result and was fortunate to win the Soil Association award for it.

A

B

160 g/⅔ cup white sourdough starter (see page 11)

300 g/300 ml/1¼ cups whey (drained from 1 litre/quart plain yogurt) or buttermilk

200 g/1⅔ cups white strong/bread flour

220 g/1¾ cups white strong/bread flour

8 g/1½ teaspoons salt

proofing/dough-rising basket (900-g/2-lb. capacity) or colander

proofing linen or clean tea/kitchen towel

floured bread peel and baking stone (optional)

baking sheet lined with parchment paper

MAKES 1 LARGE LOAF

1 In one (larger) mixing bowl, weigh out the sourdough starter and whey and mix with a wooden spoon until well combined.

2 Add the 200 g/1⅔ cups flour and mix well. This is the pre-ferment.

3 Cover and let ferment overnight in a cool place.

4 The next day, the pre-ferment should show little bubbles on the surface. **(A)**

5 In a (smaller) mixing bowl, mix the 220 g/1¾ cups flour and salt together. This is the dry mixture.

6 Add the dry mixture to the pre-ferment and mix until it comes together.

7 Cover with the bowl that had the dry mixture in it.

8 Let stand for 10 minutes.

9 After 10 minutes, knead the dough as in Step 5 on page 87.

10 Cover the bowl again and let stand for a further 10 minutes.

11 Repeat Steps 9 and 10 twice, then Step 9 again. **(B)**

12 Cover the bowl and let rise for 1 hour.

13 Lightly dust a clean work surface with flour. Put the dough on the work surface.

14 Shape the dough into a smooth, rounded disc.

15 Line a proofing/dough-rising basket or a colander with proofing linen or a clean tea/kitchen towel. Dust liberally with flour and lay the dough inside it. **(C)**

16 Let rise until about double the size – this will take between 3 and 6 hours. **(D)**

17 About 20 minutes before baking, preheat the oven to 240°C (475°F) Gas 9. Place a roasting pan at the bottom of the oven to preheat. Fill a cup with water and set aside.

18 When the dough has doubled in volume, tip it out of the basket or colander onto the bread peel or prepared baking sheet.

19 Gently peel away the linen or towel. **(E)**

20 Slash a leaf pattern on the surface of the bread using a sharp, serrated knife. **(F)**

21 Slide the bread into the preheated oven on its baking sheet, or if using a baking stone, slide it from the peel onto the hot stone. Pour the reserved cupful of water onto the hot roasting pan and lower the oven temperature to 220°C (425°F) Gas 7.

22 Bake for about 30 minutes, or until golden.

23 To check if the bread is baked through, tip it upside down and tap the bottom – it should sound hollow.

24 If it is not ready, return to the oven for a few minutes. If it is ready, set it on a wire rack to cool.

C

D

E

F

A   B   C

SOURDOUGH GRISSINI

Grissini are great for dipping and generally make a good snack or savoury treat to serve with a pre-dinner drink. I discovered a version of this recipe in Italy and converted it to use sourdough. I like the slightly unusual sour flavour of the grissini, as well as the pleasing snapping sound they make when you break them in two.

200 g/1⅔ cups white strong/bread flour or Italian "00" flour

4 g/¾ teaspoon salt

100 g/⅓ cup white sourdough starter (see page 11)

110 g/110 ml/scant ½ cup warm water

20 g/20 ml/1 tablespoon plus 1 teaspoon olive oil

baking sheets lined with parchment paper

MAKES 12–15 GRISSINI

1 In one (smaller) mixing bowl, mix the flour and salt together. This is the dry mixture.

2 In another (larger) mixing bowl, mix the sourdough starter and water together until well combined. Stir in the olive oil. This is the wet mixture.

3 Add the dry mixture to the wet mixture and mix until it comes together.

4 Cover with the bowl that had the dry mixture in it and let stand for 10 minutes.

5 After 10 minutes, knead the dough as in Step 5 on page 87.

6 Cover the bowl again and let stand for 10 minutes.

7 Repeat Steps 5 and 6 twice, then Step 5 again.

8 Cover the bowl and let rise for 1 hour.

9 Lightly dust a clean work surface with flour. Put the dough on the work surface.

10 Push the dough out with your fingertips to flatten it and widen it into a rectangle 5 mm/¼ inch thick. **(A)**

11 Cover loosely with clingfilm/plastic wrap and let rest for 15 minutes.

12 After 15 minutes, use a sharp knife to cut the rectangle of dough into 1-cm/⅜-inch wide strips. **(B)**

13 Stretch each grissini to lengthen slightly and arrange on the prepared baking sheets. **(C)**

14 Let rise in a cool place for about 2 hours.

15 About 20 minutes before baking, preheat the oven to 240°C (475°F) Gas 9. Place a roasting pan at the bottom of the oven to preheat. Fill a cup with water and set aside.

16 Place the baking sheets in the preheated oven, pour the reserved cupful of water onto the hot roasting pan and lower the oven temperature to 180°C (350°F) Gas 4.

17 Bake for about 20 minutes, or until golden brown.

18 Let cool on a wire rack.

POLENTA SOURDOUGH

When I worked in Mykonos and in other parts of Greece, we were served a yellow village bread at every meal. This sourdough version is similar to a traditional Portuguese bread called *broa* and always reminds me of the sunshine in Greece and the simple, flavourful food we ate.

A

B

C

D

E   F   G   H

300 g/2⅓ cups white strong/bread flour

8 g/1½ teaspoons salt

60 g/⅓ cup cornmeal or polenta

180 g/180 ml/⅔ cup warm water

250 g/1 cup white sourdough starter (see page 11)

2 teaspoons olive oil

extra cornmeal/polenta, for dusting

proofing/dough-rising basket (900-g/2-lb. capacity) or colander

floured bread peel and baking stone (optional)

baking sheet lined with parchment paper

MAKES 1 LARGE LOAF

1 In one (smaller) mixing bowl, mix the flour and salt together. This is the dry mixture.

2 Cook the cornmeal or polenta according to the manufacturer's instructions. **(A)**

3 Take the pan off the heat and spoon the hot polenta into a (larger) mixing bowl. You need 150 g/ 5 oz. cooked polenta, so check the weight now and take out any excess.

4 Add the water to the polenta and stir. Make sure you do this while the polenta is still hot or warm and don't worry if there are a few small lumps – this will add to the texture. **(B)**

5 Add the sourdough starter and olive oil to the polenta mixture and mix until well combined. This is the wet mixture. **(C)**

6 Add the dry mixture to the wet mixture and mix by hand until it comes together.

7 Cover with the bowl that had the dry mixture in it.

8 Let stand for 10 minutes.

9 After 10 minutes, knead the dough as in Step 5 on page 87.

10 Cover the bowl again and let stand for a further 10 minutes.

11 Repeat Steps 9 and 10 twice, then Step 9 again. **(D)**

12 Cover the bowl and let rise for 1 hour.

13 Lightly dust a clean work surface with cornmeal or polenta. Put the dough on the work surface.

14 Shape the dough into a smooth, rounded disc, coating it all over in the cornmeal or polenta.

15 Dust the proofing/dough-rising basket with flour. Lay the dough inside it.

16 Let the dough rise until about double the size – this will take between 3 and 6 hours. **(E)**

17 About 20 minutes before baking, preheat the oven to 240°C (475°F) Gas 9. Place a roasting pan at the bottom of the oven to preheat. Fill a cup with water and set aside.

18 When the dough has doubled in volume, tip it out of the basket onto the bread peel or prepared baking sheet. **(F) (G)**

19 Slash a parallel lines on the surface of the bread using a sharp, serrated knife. **(H)**

20 Slide the bread into the preheated oven on its baking sheet, or if using a baking stone, slide it from the peel onto the hot stone. Pour the reserved cupful of water onto the hot roasting pan and lower the oven temperature to 220°C (425°F) Gas 7.

21 Bake for about 30 minutes, or until brown.

22 To check if the bread is baked through, tip it upside down and tap the bottom – it should sound hollow.

23 Set it on a wire rack to cool.

A   B   C

TOMATO SOURDOUGH BREAD

The tomato purée or paste in this bread dough gives the baked crumb its great orange colour. The tomato is beautifully complemented by the celery and nigella seeds. If you don't like celery, replace it with freshly chopped rosemary, which works nicely, too.

400 g/3⅓ cups white strong/bread flour

10 g/2 teaspoons salt

4 g/¾ teaspoon celery seeds or 2½ tablespoons freshly chopped rosemary leaves

6 g/1¼ teaspoons nigella seeds (black onion seeds)

40 g/2½ tablespoons tomato purée/paste

200 g/200 ml/¾ cup warm water

300 g/1¼ cups white sourdough starter (see page 11)

2 teaspoons olive oil

long proofing/dough-rising basket (900-g/ 2-lb. capacity)

floured bread peel and baking stone (optional)

baking sheet lined with parchment paper

MAKES 1 LARGE LOAF

1 In one (smaller) mixing bowl, mix the flour, salt and seeds together. This is the dry mixture.

2 In another (larger) mixing bowl, mix the tomato purée/paste and water together until well combined. Stir in the sourdough starter. **(A)**

3 Add the olive oil and mix. This is the wet mixture.

4 Add the dry mixture to the wet mixture and mix until it comes together.

5 Cover with the bowl that had the dry mixture in it

6 Let stand for 10 minutes.

7 After 10 minutes, knead the dough as in Step 5 on page 87.

8 Cover the bowl again and let stand for 10 minutes.

9 Repeat Steps 7 and 8 twice, then Step 7 again.

10 Cover the bowl and let rise for 1 hour.

11 Lightly dust a clean work surface with flour. Put the dough on the work surface and shape it with your hands, in the flour, until it is roughly the length and width of your proofing/dough-rising basket.

12 Sprinkle flour in the proofing/dough-rising basket and lay the bread inside it.

13 Let the dough rise until about double the size – this will take between 3 and 6 hours. **(B)**

14 About 20 minutes before baking, preheat the oven to 240°C (475°F) Gas 9. Place a roasting pan at the bottom of the oven to preheat. Fill a cup with water and set aside.

15 When the dough has doubled in volume, tip it out of the basket onto the bread peel or prepared baking sheet.

16 Slash a straight line down the middle of the bread using a sharp, serrated knife. **(C)**

17 Slide the bread into the preheated oven on its baking sheet, or if using a baking stone, slide it from the peel onto the hot stone. Pour the reserved cupful of water onto the hot roasting pan and lower the oven temperature to 220°C (425°F) Gas 7.

18 Bake for about 30 minutes, or until brown.

19 To check if the bread is baked through, tip it upside down and tap the bottom – it should sound hollow.

20 If it is not ready, return to the oven for a few minutes. If it is ready, set it on a wire rack to cool.

A

B

C

D

BEETROOT SOURDOUGH

What I love about this bread is the sweet, earthy smell it gets from the beetroot/beets, not to mention the colour of the raw dough, which is bright purple. The trick is to grate the beets coarsely so that they retain their colour and don't melt into the dough when the bread is baked. The result is a fantastic polka-dot finish to the crumb – a great talking point at a dinner party!

370 g/3 cups white strong/bread flour

8 g/1½ teaspoons salt

160 g/5½ oz. fresh raw beetroot/beets, scrubbed clean

220 g/1 scant cup white sourdough starter (see page 11)

200 g/200 ml/¾ cup warm water

10 g/2 teaspoons olive oil

proofing/dough-rising basket (900-g/2-lb. capacity) (optional)

floured bread peel and baking stone

baking sheet lined with parchment paper

MAKES 1 LARGE LOAF

1 In one (smaller) mixing bowl, mix the flour and salt together. This is the dry mixture.

2 Coarsely grate the beetroot/beets and set aside. **(A)**

3 In another (larger) mixing bowl, mix the sourdough starter and water together until well combined. Now add the olive oil. This is the wet mixture.

4 Add the dry mixture to the wet mixture and mix with your hands until it comes together, then mix in the grated beetroot/beets until well combined.

5 Cover with the bowl that had the dry mixture in it and let stand for 10 minutes.

6 After 10 minutes, knead the dough as in Step 5 on page 87.

7 Cover the bowl again and let stand for 10 minutes.

8 Repeat Steps 6 and 7 twice, then Step 6 again. **(B)**

9 Cover the bowl and let rise for 1 hour.

10 Lightly dust a clean work surface with flour. Put the dough on the work surface.

11 Shape the dough into a smooth, rounded disc.

12 Dust the proofing/dough-rising basket with flour. Lay the dough inside it and dust the dough with flour.

13 Let the dough rise until about double the size – this will take between 3 and 6 hours. **(C)**

14 About 20 minutes before baking, preheat the oven to 240°C (475°F) Gas 9. Place a roasting pan at the bottom of the oven to preheat. Fill a cup with water and set aside.

15 When the dough has doubled in volume, tip it out of the basket onto the bread peel or prepared baking sheet. **(D)**

16 Slide the bread into the preheated oven on its baking sheet, or if using a baking stone, slide it from the peel onto the hot stone. Pour the reserved cupful of water onto the hot roasting pan and lower the oven temperature to 220°C (425°F) Gas 7.

17 Bake the bread for about 30 minutes, or until golden brown.

18 To check if the bread is baked through, tip it upside down and tap the bottom – it should sound hollow.

19 If it is not ready, return to the oven for a few minutes. If it is ready, set it on a wire rack to cool.

A

B

C

SPICED CHEESE AND HERB SOURDOUGH

When I was at Daylesford, the cheese maker Joe made a great chilli cheddar cheese with the chillies grown by Ben the gardener at the time. I decided to make a bread using chilli that is full of flavour and in my opinion should just be eaten as it is with great butter.

300 g/2½ cups white strong/bread flour

8 g/2 teaspoons salt

2 g/⅓ teaspoon ground chilli powder or (hot pepper) flakes

150 g/1½ cups coarsely grated cheddar cheese

4 tablespoons freshly chopped coriander/cilantro or parsley

200 g/1 scant cup white sourdough starter (see page 11)

180 g/180 ml/⅔ cup warm water

4 small proofing/dough-rising baskets

floured bread peel and baking stone (optional)

baking sheet lined with parchment paper

MAKES 4 MINI LOAVES

1 In one (smaller) mixing bowl, mix the flour, salt and chilli powder or flakes together. This is the dry mixture.

2 Mix the cheese and herbs together.

3 In another (larger) mixing bowl, mix the sourdough starter and water together until well combined. This is the wet mixture.

4 Add the dry mixture and the cheese mixture to the wet mixture and mix with your hands until it comes together. (A)

5 Cover with the bowl that had the dry mixture in it and let stand for 10 minutes.

6 After 10 minutes, knead the dough as in Step 5 on page 87.

7 Cover the bowl again and let stand for 10 minutes.

8 Repeat Steps 6 and 7 twice and then Step 6 again.

9 Cover the bowl and let rise for 1 hour.

10 Lightly dust a clean work surface with flour. Put the dough on the work surface.

11 Divide the dough into 4 equal portions using a metal dough scraper or sharp, serrated knife. If you want to be as accurate as possible, weigh each piece and add or subtract dough from the portions until they all weigh the same.

12 Shape the portions of dough into smooth, rounded discs.

13 Dust the proofing/dough-rising baskets with flour. Lay a portion of dough inside each one. (B)

14 Let the dough rise until about double the size – this will take between 3 and 6 hours.

15 About 20 minutes before baking, preheat the oven to 240°C (475°F) Gas 9. Place a roasting pan at the bottom of the oven to preheat. Fill a cup with water and set aside.

16 When the dough has doubled in volume, tip it out of the baskets onto the bread peel or prepared baking sheet. Slash 2 curved incisions on the surface of the loaves using a sharp, serrated knife. (C)

17 Slide the breads into the preheated oven on the baking sheet, or if using a baking stone, slide them from the peel onto the hot stone. Pour the reserved cupful of water onto the hot roasting pan and lower the oven temperature to 220°C (425°F) Gas 7.

18 Bake for about 30 minutes, or until golden brown.

19 To check if the bread is baked through, tip one loaf upside down and tap the bottom – it should sound hollow.

20 If they are not ready, return to the oven for a few minutes. If they are ready, set on a wire rack to cool.

A
B
C
D
E
F
G
H
I
J
K
L
M

POTATO SOURDOUGH

A classic American-style bread with raw, baked or roasted potato, which makes for a great crust. This makes fantastic toast.

250 g/1 cup white sourdough starter (see page 11)

180 g/180 ml/⅔ cup warm water

10 g/2 teaspoons olive oil

310 g/2½ cups white strong/bread flour

6 g/1 teaspoon salt

150 g/5 oz. raw peeled potatoes, coarsely grated, or skin-on roasted potatoes, broken into pieces

proofing/dough-rising basket (500-g/1-lb. capacity)

floured bread peel and baking stone (optional)

baking sheet lined with parchment paper

MAKES 1 SMALL LOAF

1 In one (larger) mixing bowl, mix the sourdough starter and water together until well combined. Stir in the olive oil. This is the wet mixture. **(A)**

2 In another (smaller) mixing bowl, mix the flour, salt and potato together. This is the dry mixture. **(B)**

3 Add the dry mixture to the wet mixture. **(C)**

4 Mix with your hands until it comes together. **(D)**

5 Cover with the bowl that had the dry mixture in it and let stand for 10 minutes.

6 After 10 minutes, knead the dough as in Step 5 on page 87. **(E)**

7 Cover the bowl again and let stand for 10 minutes.

8 Repeat Steps 6 and 7 twice and then Step 6 again. **(F)**

9 Cover the bowl and let rise for 1 hour.

10 Lightly dust a clean work surface with flour. Put the dough on the work surface and dust it lightly with flour. **(G)**

11 Shape the dough into a smooth, rounded disc. **(H) (I)**

12 Dust the proofing/dough-rising basket with flour and lay the dough inside it. **(J)**

13 Let the dough rise until about double the size – this will take between 3 and 6 hours. **(K)**

14 About 20 minutes before baking, preheat the oven to 240°C (475°F) Gas 9. Place a roasting pan at the bottom of the oven to preheat. Fill a cup with water and set aside.

15 When the dough has doubled in volume, tip it out of the basket onto the bread peel or prepared baking sheet. **(L)**

16 Slide the bread into the preheated oven on the baking sheet, or if using a baking stone, slide it from the peel onto the hot stone. Pour the reserved cupful of water onto the hot roasting pan and lower the oven temperature to 220°C (425°F) Gas 7.

17 Bake for about 30 minutes, or until golden brown. **(M: shows one bread made with raw, grated potato and the another made with roasted potato.)**

18 To check if the bread is baked through, tip it upside down and tap the bottom – it should sound hollow.

19 If it is not ready, return to the oven for a few minutes. If it is ready, set it on a wire rack to cool.

FIG, WALNUT AND ANISE SOURDOUGH

Fig and walnut is such a wonderful combination, and the subtle addition of star anise is lovely. Try this bread with cheese for a novel accompaniment.

3 plump dried figs, roughly chopped

40 g/⅓ cup chopped walnuts

2 g/½ teaspoon ground star anise

100 g/¾ cup white strong/bread flour

45 g/⅓ cup wholemeal/
whole-wheat flour

20 g/2½ tablespoons dark rye/
pumpernickel flour

3 g/½ teaspoon salt

65 g/¼ cup white sourdough starter
(see page 11)

130 g/130 ml/½ cup warm water

*long proofing/dough-rising basket
(900-g/2-lb. capacity)*

*floured bread peel and baking stone
(optional)*

*baking sheet lined with parchment
paper*

MAKES 1 SMALL LOAF

1 Mix the figs, nuts and anise and set aside.

2 In one (smaller) mixing bowl, mix the flours and salt together. This is the dry mixture.

3 In a (larger) mixing bowl, mix the sourdough starter and water together until well combined. This is the wet mixture.

4 Add the dry mixture and fig mixture to the wet mixture and mix until it comes together.

5 Cover with the bowl that had the dry mixture in it and let stand for 10 minutes.

6 After 10 minutes, knead the dough as in Step 5 on page 87.

7 Cover the bowl again and let stand for 10 minutes.

8 Repeat Steps 6 and 7 twice, then Step 6 again. Cover the bowl again and let rise for 1 hour. **(A)**

9 When the dough has doubled in volume, punch it down with your fist to release the air.

10 Lightly dust a clean work surface with flour. Transfer the ball of dough to the floured work surface.

11 Fold one edge of the dough over into the middle. Fold the opposite edge over to the middle. Now roll the dough to make a sausage. Make the ends tapered.

12 Dust the proofing/dough-rising basket with flour. Lay the dough inside it. **(B)**

13 Let the dough rise until about double the size – this will take between 3 and 6 hours.

14 About 20 minutes before baking, preheat the oven to 240°C (475°F) Gas 9. Place a roasting pan at the bottom of the oven to preheat. Fill a cup with water and set aside.

15 When the dough has doubled in volume, tip it out of the basket onto the bread peel or prepared baking sheet. Sprinkle flour over the bread. Slash diagonal lines along the surface using a sharp, serrated knife. **(C)**

16 Slide the bread into the preheated oven on the baking sheet, or if using a baking stone, slide it from the peel onto the hot stone. Pour the reserved cupful of water onto the hot roasting pan and lower the oven temperature to 220°C (425°F) Gas 7.

17 Bake for about 30 minutes, or until golden brown. Let cool on a wire rack.

A   B   C

HAZELNUT AND CURRANT SOURDOUGH

The most important element in this bread is the lightly toasted hazelnuts. Toasting them brings out their flavour and complements the sweet currants. Try this bread with cheese.

120 g/1 cup lightly toasted hazelnuts, chopped
60 g/½ cup (Zante) currants
375 g/3 cups white strong/bread flour
6 g/1 teaspoon salt
140 g/⅗ cup white sourdough starter (see page 11)
250 g/250 ml/1 cup warm water

proofing/dough-rising basket (900-g/2-lb. capacity) or colander
proofing linen or clean tea/kitchen towel
floured bread peel and baking stone (optional)
baking sheet lined with parchment paper

MAKES 1 LARGE LOAF

A

1 Mix the nuts and currants and set aside.

2 In one (smaller) mixing bowl, mix the flour and salt together. This is the dry mixture.

3 In a (larger) mixing bowl, mix the sourdough starter and water together until well combined. This is the wet mixture.

4 Add the dry mixture and nut mixture to the wet mixture and mix until it comes together.

5 Cover with the bowl that had the dry mixture in it and let stand for 10 minutes.

6 After 10 minutes, knead the dough as in Step 5 on page 87.

7 Cover the bowl again and let stand for 10 minutes.

8 Repeat Steps 6 and 7 twice, then Step 6 again. **(A)**

9 Cover the bowl and let rise for 1 hour.

10 Lightly dust a clean work surface with flour. Put the dough on the work surface and shape into a smooth, rounded disc.

11 Line a proofing/dough-rising basket or a colander with proofing linen or a clean tea/kitchen towel. Dust liberally with flour and lay the dough inside it.

12 Let rise until about double the size – this will take between 3 and 6 hours. **(B)**

13 About 20 minutes before baking, preheat the oven to 240°C (475°F) Gas 9. Place a roasting pan at the bottom of the oven to preheat. Fill a cup with water and set aside.

14 When the dough has doubled in volume, tip it out of the basket or colander onto the bread peel or prepared baking sheet. Gently peel away the linen or towel. **(C) (D)**

15 Slash simple lines on the surface of the bread using a sharp, serrated knife.

16 Slide the bread into the preheated oven on its baking sheet, or if using a baking stone, slide it from the peel onto the hot stone. Pour the reserved cupful of water onto the hot roasting pan and lower the oven temperature to 220°C (425°F) Gas 7.

17 Bake for about 30 minutes, or until golden.

18 To check if the bread is baked through, tip it upside down and tap the bottom – it should sound hollow.

19 If it is not ready, return to the oven for a few minutes. If it is ready, set it on a wire rack to cool.

CHOCOLATE AND CURRANT SOURDOUGH

I love this bread with its deep chocolate flavour. I decided to add the currants, as it provided a sweet counterpoint to the rich cocoa. This is such a magical and unexpectedly good loaf that it would make a lovely gift for a foodie friend.

200 g/1⅓ cups (Zante) currants

80 g/⅔ cup milk/semi-sweet chocolate chips

330 g/2⅔ cups white strong/bread flour

8 g/1½ teaspoons salt

20 g/2½ tablespoons cocoa powder

170 g/⅔ cup white sourdough starter (see page 11)

250 g/250 ml/1 cup warm water

long proofing/dough-rising basket (900-g/2-lb. capacity)

floured bread peel and baking stone (optional)

baking sheet lined with parchment paper

MAKES 1 LARGE LOAF

1 Mix the currants and chocolate and set aside.

2 In one (smaller) mixing bowl, mix the flour, salt and cocoa powder together. This is the dry mixture.

3 In a (larger) mixing bowl, mix the sourdough starter and water together until well combined. This is the wet mixture.

4 Add the dry mixture and chocolate mixture to the wet mixture and mix until it comes together.

5 Cover with the bowl that had the dry mixture in it and let stand for 10 minutes.

6 After 10 minutes, knead the dough as in Step 5 on page 87.

7 Cover the bowl again and let stand for 10 minutes.

8 Repeat Steps 6 and 7 twice, then Step 6 again. Cover the bowl again and let rise for 1 hour. **(A)**

9 When the dough has doubled in volume, punch it down with your fist to release the air.

10 Lightly dust a clean work surface with flour. Transfer the ball of dough to the floured work surface.

11 Divide the dough into 2 equal portions and roll each one into a ball.

12 Dust the proofing/dough-rising basket with flour. Lay the 2 balls of dough inside it, side by side, so that they fit snugly together. **(B)**

13 Let the dough rise until about double the size – this will take between 3 and 6 hours.

14 About 20 minutes before baking, preheat the oven to 240°C (475°F) Gas 9. Place a roasting pan at the bottom of the oven to preheat. Fill a cup with water and set aside.

15 When the dough has doubled in volume, tip it out of the basket onto the bread peel or prepared baking sheet. Sprinkle flour over the bread. Slash crosses on the surface using a sharp, serrated knife. **(C)**

16 Slide the bread into the preheated oven on the baking sheet, or if using a baking stone, slide it from the peel onto the hot stone. Pour the reserved cupful of water onto the hot roasting pan and lower the oven temperature to 220°C (425°F) Gas 7.

17 Bake for about 30 minutes, or until brown.

18 To check if the bread is baked through, tip it upside down and tap the bottom – it should sound hollow. Let cool on a wire rack.

A   B   C

CARAWAY RYE SOURDOUGH

In my mind, this is a classic rye bread of the type that you find in Germany, with the slight hint of caraway. It looks fabulous when its baked because the crust cracks dramatically.

350 g/3 cups dark rye/pumpernickel flour

150 g/1½ cups white strong/bread flour

10 g/2 teaspoons salt

3 g/1 generous teaspoon caraway seeds

250 g/1 cup rye sourdough starter (see page 11)

400 g/400 ml/1½ cups warm water

proofing/dough-rising basket (900-g/2-lb. capacity)

floured bread peel and baking stone (optional)

baking sheet lined with parchment paper

MAKES 1 LARGE LOAF

D

E

1 In one (smaller) mixing bowl, mix the flours, salt and seeds together. This is the dry mixture. **(A)**

2 In another (larger) mixing bowl, mix the sourdough starter and water together until well combined. This is the wet mixture. **(B)**

3 Add the dry mixture to the wet mixture and mix until it comes together and looks like thick porridge. **(C) (D)**

4 Cover with the bowl that had the dry mixture in it and let stand for 1 hour.

5 After 1 hour, transfer the dough to a lightly floured surface and shape roughly into a disc.

6 Generously dust a tray with dark rye/pumpernickel flour.

7 Roll the dough in the flour. **(E)**

8 Dust the proofing/dough-rising basket with flour. Lay the dough inside it and dust the dough with flour. **(F) (G)**

9 Let the dough rise until about double the size – this will take between 3 and 6 hours. **(H)**

10 About 20 minutes before baking, preheat the oven to 240°C (475°F) Gas 9. Place a roasting pan at the bottom of the oven to preheat. Fill a cup with water and set aside.

11 When the dough has doubled in volume, tip it out of the basket onto the bread peel or prepared baking sheet. **(I)**

12 Slide the bread into the preheated oven on its baking sheet, or if using a baking stone, slide it from the peel onto the hot stone. Pour the reserved cupful of water onto the hot roasting pan and lower the oven temperature to 230°C (450°F) Gas 8.

13 Bake for about 30 minutes, or until brown.

14 To check if the bread is baked through, tip it upside down and tap the bottom – it should sound hollow.

15 If it is not ready, return to the oven for a few minutes. If it is ready, set it on a wire rack to cool.

F

G

H

I

3-GRAIN BREAD

I made this as an apprentice at Zerbans Cake and Coffee Shop in Cape Town. It is packed with rye, wheat and oats, plus lots of seeds.

2 tablespoons each of fennel and coriander seeds, plus 1 tablespoon caraway seeds, for a spice blend

100 g/100 ml/½ cup cold water

50 g/⅓ cup sunflower seeds

30 g/⅕ cup linseed/flaxseed

12 g/2 tablespoons porridge/old-fashioned rolled oats

12 g/2 tablespoons chopped/cracked wheat

180 g/¾ cup rye sourdough starter (see page 11)

150 g/150 ml/⅔ cup warm water

250 g/2 cups light rye flour

150 g/1¼ cups white strong/bread flour

8 g/1½ teaspoons salt

4 g fresh yeast or 2 g/½ teaspoon dried/active dry yeast

50 g/50 ml/3 tablespoons warm water

long proofing/dough-rising basket (900-g/ 2-lb. capacity)

floured bread peel and baking stone (optional)

baking sheet lined with parchment paper

MAKES 1 LARGE LOAF

1 To make a spice blend, mix the fennel, coriander and caraway seeds and toast in a dry saucepan over low heat until the seeds pop. Let cool, then grind with a pestle and mortar or spice grinder.

2 Put the 100 g/100 ml/½ cup water, the sunflower seeds, linseed/flaxseed, oats and chopped/cracked wheat in a (larger) mixing bowl and stir. This is the wet mixture. Cover and set aside in a cool place overnight.

3 At the same time, in another (larger) mixing bowl, mix the sourdough starter and the 150 g/150 ml/⅔ cup warm water together until well combined. Add the light rye flour and mix to a paste. Cover and let ferment in a cool place overnight.

4 The next day, in a (smaller) mixing bowl, mix the white flour, salt and 1 teaspoon of the spice blend together. This is the dry mixture.

5 In a (smaller) bowl, dissolve the yeast in the 50 g/50 ml/ 3 tablespoons warm water, then add to the fermented sourdough mixture and mix well.

6 Now mix in the wet mixture and the dry mixture until it all comes together. The mixture should be quite stiff and sticky, but if it looks too dry, add a little water.

7 Cover with the bowl that had the dry mixture in it and let stand for 10 minutes.

8 After 10 minutes, knead the dough as in Step 5 on page 87. It will be quite sticky.

9 Cover the bowl again and let stand for 10 minutes.

10 Repeat Steps 8 and 9 twice, then Step 8 again. **(A)**

11 Cover the bowl again and let rise for 1 hour. **(B)**

12 Lightly dust a clean work surface with oats. Transfer the ball of dough to the work surface. **(C)**

13 Shape it with your hands, in the oats, until it is roughly the length and width of your proofing basket. **(D)**

14 Sprinkle more oats in the proofing basket and lay the bread inside it.

15 Let the dough rise until about double the size – 1–2 hours. **(E)**

16 About 20 minutes before baking, preheat the oven to 240°C (475°F) Gas 9. Place a roasting pan at the bottom of the oven to preheat. Fill a cup with water and set aside.

17 When the dough has doubled in volume, tip it out of the basket onto the bread peel or prepared baking sheet. Slash a zigzag on the surface using a sharp, serrated knife. **(F)**

18 Slide the bread into the preheated oven on the baking sheet, or if using a baking stone, slide it from the peel onto the hot stone. Pour the reserved cupful of water onto the hot roasting pan and lower the oven temperature to 220°C (425°F) Gas 7.

19 Bake for about 30 minutes, or until brown.

20 Let cool on a wire rack.

SEMOLINA BREAD

This is my take on the Italian semolina bread from Altamira. I have made it this way to break down the semolina and create a subtle and delicately sweet taste. The bread is very versatile and marries well with almost anything you choose to put on it.

125 g/1 cup white
strong/bread flour
or Italian "00" flour

3 g/½ teaspoon salt

25 g/2 tablespoons
white sourdough starter
(see page 11)

150 g/150 ml/⅝ cup
warm water

150 g/1 cup plus
2 tablespoons semolina

3 g fresh yeast
or 2 g/¾ teaspoon
dried/active dry yeast

50 g/50 ml/3
tablespoons warm water

5 g/1 teaspoon olive oil

15 g/3 teaspoons olive
oil

*baking sheet lined with
parchment paper*

MAKES 1 SMALL LOAF

1 In a (smaller) mixing bowl, mix the flour and salt together. This is the dry mixture.

2 In one (larger) mixing bowl, weigh out the sourdough starter, the 150 g/150 ml/⅝ cup water and semolina. **(A)**

3 Mix with a wooden spoon until well mixed. **(B)**

4 Cover and let ferment for 2 hours or overnight in a cool place. This is the pre-ferment. **(C)**

5 When the pre-ferment is ready, in a (larger) mixing bowl, dissolve the yeast in the 50 g/50 ml/3 tablespoons water and stir in the 5 g/1 teaspoon olive oil. **(D)**

6 Mix the yeast solution into the pre-ferment. This is the wet mixture.

7 Add the dry mixture to the wet mixture. **(E)**

8 Mix with a wooden spoon until it comes together. **(F)**

9 Cover and let stand for 10 minutes. It will be very soft at this stage.

10 Pour half the 15 g/3 teaspoons olive oil into another large bowl.

11 Scrape the dough into the bowl with the olive oil using a dough scraper. **(G)**

12 Pull a portion of the dough up from the side and press it into the middle. Turn the bowl slightly and repeat this process with another portion of dough. Repeat twice. **(H)**

13 Let rest for 10 minutes. **(I)**

14 Repeat Steps 12 and 13 another 3 times, adding the rest of the olive oil so that the dough doesn't stick to the bowl. **(J)**

15 Let rest for 10 minutes.

16 Lightly dust a clean work surface with flour. Put the dough on the work surface.

17 Fold the dough as in Step 12 twice. **(K) (L) (M)**

18 Let rest for 15–20 minutes.

19 After 15–20 minutes, fold the dough again, swivelling it round, to make a circle. Flip it over and tuck in any edges so that you have a smooth, flat ball. **(N)**

20 Dust the prepared baking sheet with semolina and put the dough on it. Dust the dough with semolina. **(O)**

21 Make a hole in the middle of the dough with your fingers, then gently pull the side out until it becomes a ring. **(P)**

22 Let rise for 30 minutes, or until bubbles start to form on the surface of the dough.

23 About 20 minutes before baking, preheat the oven to 240°C (475°F) Gas 9. Place a roasting pan at the bottom of the oven to preheat. Fill a cup with water and set aside.

24 When the bread is ready to bake, score 3 lines in the surface using a sharp, serrated knife. **(Q)**

25 Slide the bread into the preheated oven. Pour the reserved cupful of water onto the hot roasting pan and lower the oven temperature to 220°C (425°F) Gas 7.

26 Bake for about 35 minutes, or until golden. **(R)**

27 To check if the bread is baked through, tip it upside down and tap the bottom – it should sound hollow.

28 If it is not ready, return to the oven for a few minutes. If it is ready, set it on a wire rack to cool.

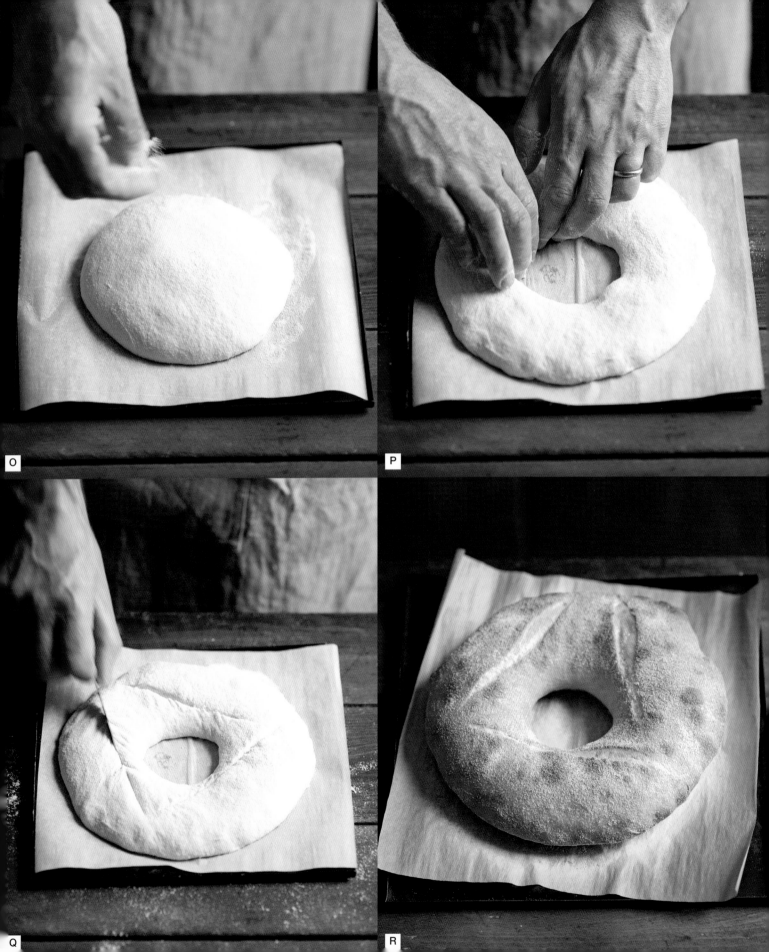

MULTIGRAIN SUNFLOWER BREAD

This is another great German-style bread packed full of so much flavour that it can be eaten just on its own. The sunflower seeds give a lovely crunch.

2 teaspoons blackstrap or dark molasses

140 g/140 ml/½ cup plus 1 tablespoon warm water

100 g/⅝ cup chopped/cracked rye

140 g/1 cup dark rye/pumpernickel flour

40 g/⅓ cup malthouse/whole-wheat flour

10 g/2 teaspoons salt

100 g/⅔ cup sunflower seeds

6 g fresh yeast or 3 g/1 teaspoon dried/active dry yeast

80 g/80 ml/⅓ cup warm water

60 g/¼ cup rye sourdough starter (see page 11)

500-g/6 x 4-in. loaf pan, greased with vegetable oil

MAKES 1 MEDIUM LOAF

1 In one (larger) mixing bowl, dissolve the molasses in the 140 g/140 ml/½ cup plus 1 tablespoon water.

2 Add the chopped/cracked rye and stir. Cover and let soak until soft – overnight if necessary.

3 In another (larger) mixing bowl, mix the flours, salt and seeds together and set aside. This is the dry mixture.

4 In another (smaller) bowl, dissolve the yeast in the 80 g/80 ml/⅓ cup water, then stir in the sourdough starter. This is the wet mixture.

5 Mix the wet mixture into the soaked chopped/cracked rye. Now add the dry mixture. **(A)**

6 Stir with a wooden spoon until well mixed. **(B)**

7 Cover with the bowl that had the dry mixture in it and let stand for 1 hour.

8 Spoon the mixture into the prepared loaf pan. Dip a plastic scraper or tablespoon in water and use to smooth the surface of the dough. **(C)**

9 Cover the loaf and let rise for 30–45 minutes. **(D)**

10 About 20 minutes before baking, preheat the oven to 240°C (475°F) Gas 9. Place a roasting pan at the bottom of the oven to preheat. Fill a cup with water and set aside.

11 Slide the bread into the preheated oven. Pour the reserved cupful of water onto the hot roasting pan and lower the oven temperature to 220°C (425°F) Gas 7.

12 Bake for about 35 minutes, or until brown.

13 Let cool on a wire rack.

PASTRIES & SWEET TREATS

CROISSANTS

Once you have mastered the method for making *croissants*, you can recreate your own little French café and bake *pains au chocolat* and *pains aux raisins*, too.

250 g/2 cups white strong/bread flour

20 g/1½ tablespoons (caster) sugar

5 g/1 teaspoon salt

10 g fresh yeast or 5 g/1½ teaspoons dried/ active dry yeast

125 g/125 ml/½ cup warm water

150 g/10 tablespoons butter, slightly soft

1 medium egg, beaten with a pinch of salt, for the egg wash

baking sheet lined with parchment paper

MAKES ABOUT 8

1 In one (smaller) mixing bowl, mix the flour, sugar and salt together. This is the dry mixture.

2 In another (larger) mixing bowl, dissolve the yeast in the water. This is the wet mixture.

3 Add the dry mixture to the wet mixture and mix until it comes together.

4 Cover with the bowl that had the dry mixture in it.

5 Let stand for 10 minutes.

6 After 10 minutes, the dough is ready to be kneaded. Leaving it in the bowl, pull a portion of the dough up from the side and press it into the middle. Turn the bowl slightly and repeat this process with another portion of dough. Repeat another 8 times. The whole process should only take about 10 seconds and the dough should start to resist.

7 Cover the bowl again and let stand for 10 minutes.

8 Now repeat Steps 6 and 7 twice. Repeat Step 6 one last time.

9 Cover and let rest in the refrigerator overnight. If you are using dried/active dry yeast, let the dough to rise for another 30 minutes at room temperature before putting it into the refrigerator overnight. This will give the yeast a kick-start.

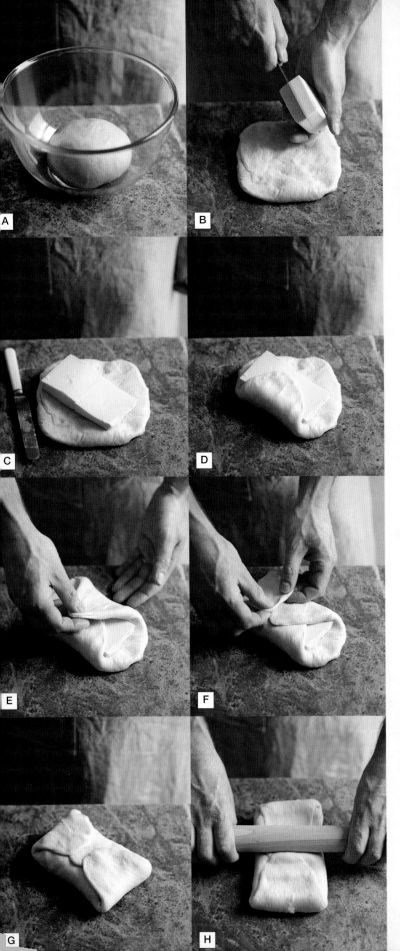

10 Remove the dough from the refrigerator. **(A)**

11 Turn the dough out onto the work surface.

12 Pull the dough outward from the edges until you have a rough square about 12 cm/5 inches.

13 Cut the butter to achieve a rectangle roughly half the size of your square of dough. **(B)**

14 Make sure the dough is about the same thickness as the rectangle of butter.

15 Place the butter diagonally across the middle of the square of dough. **(C)**

16 Fold the corners of the dough toward the middle so that they envelop the butter and you get a neat package. Stretch the dough if necessary to completely encase the butter. **(D) (E) (F) (G)**

17 Press down on the dough using a rolling pin to distribute the butter evenly through it inside the envelope. **(H)**

18 Start rolling the dough lengthwise until you have a long rectangle about 1 cm/½ inch thick. **(I)**

19 Fold the bottom third of the rectangle over. **(J)**

20 Fold the top third over. **(K)**

21 You should now have 3 rectangular pieces of dough piled on top of each other; this is your first turn. Make a small indentation into the dough with your fingertip to remind you that you have made one turn. **(L)**

22 Wrap the dough in clingfilm/plastic wrap and refrigerate for 20 minutes.

23 Remove the dough from the refrigerator and repeat Steps 17–21 twice.

24 You will now have given the pastry 3 turns and should have 3 indentations.

25 Wrap the dough in clingfilm/plastic wrap and refrigerate for 40 minutes.

26 Remove the dough from the refrigerator and roll out to a rectangle about 24 x 38 cm/10 x 15 inches. **(M)**

27 Cut the rectangle into long, thin triangles, as shown. You should have 8–9 triangles. **(N)**

28 Roll up each triangle, starting from the shortest side, into a croissant. **(O) (P)**

29 Place the croissants on the prepared baking sheets, allowing a little space between them so that they have room to rise.

30 Let rise until you see the folds in the pastry separating.

31 Preheat the oven to 240°C (475°F) Gas 9. Place a roasting pan at the bottom of the oven. Fill a cup with water.

32 When the croissants are ready to be baked, brush them lightly all over with the egg wash. **(Q)**

33 Place the baking sheets in the preheated oven, pour the reserved cupful of water onto the hot roasting pan and lower the oven temperature to 220°C (425°F) Gas 7.

34 Bake for about 15–20 minutes, or until golden brown. Don't worry if you see butter seeping out of the croissants during baking – it should all be absorbed when the croissants cool.

35 Let the croissants cool slightly on wire racks before eating.

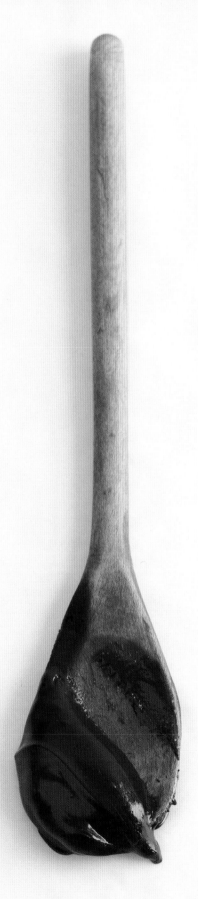

FOR THE CHOCOLATE BATONS

75 g/2½ oz. dark/bittersweet chocolate (70% cocoa solids)

1½ tablespoons water

2 tablespoons sugar

piping bag fitted with a small plain nozzle/tip

baking sheet lined with parchment paper

PAINS AU CHOCOLAT

It is worth bearing in mind that these cannot be rustled up in a couple of hours. But the best things are worth waiting for, and you will certainly be well rewarded with these French breakfast favourites.

To make the chocolate batons

1 Break or chop the chocolate into little pieces. Set aside.

2 Put the water and sugar in a saucepan and bring to a boil.

3 Once the mixture has boiled, take the saucepan off the heat.

4 Add the chocolate to the hot sugar syrup and stir until melted, smooth and shiny.

5 Let cool, stirring from time to time with a wooden spoon.

6 If the mixture is lumpy, place it over low heat, stirring continually until smooth.

7 Once the mixture has set to a piping consistency, spoon it into the piping bag and pipe into long strips about 5 mm/¼ inch thick on the prepared baking sheet. **(A)**

8 Refrigerate until ready to use. (Freeze if you don't plan to use for a while.)

B

C

D

1 quantity Croissant dough (see page 137, up to end of Step 25)

1 quantity Chocolate Batons (see page 141)

1 medium egg, beaten with a pinch of salt, for the egg wash

baking sheet lined with parchment paper

MAKES 8

1 Remove the croissant dough from the refrigerator and roll out, using a rolling pin, to a rectangle about 15 x 48 cm/6 x 20 inches.

2 Now cut the dough into 8 rectangles each measuring 15 x 6 cm/6 x 2½ inches. **(B)**

3 Break the chocolate batons with your fingers so that they are just under 6 cm/2½ inches long. You will need 16 short lengths of baton, so place the rest in the freezer for another time.

4 Place one short length of baton at the bottom of one rectangle of dough.

5 Fold the dough over the baton, then start to roll up, but only about one quarter of the way up.

6 Now place another baton on the dough immediately after the roll. **(C)**

7 Finish rolling up the dough. Making sure the seam is exactly underneath the roll of dough, flatten slightly with your hand.

8 Repeat this process with the remaining rectangles of dough to make 8 pains au chocolat.

9 Place the pains au chocolat on the prepared baking sheet, allowing a little space between them so that they have room to rise.

10 Let the pains au chocolat rise until you see the folds in the pastry separating.

11 Preheat the oven to 240°C (475°F) Gas 9. Place a roasting pan at the bottom of the oven. Fill a cup with water.

12 When the pains au chocolat are ready to be baked, brush them lightly all over with the egg wash. **(D)**

13 Place the baking sheet in the preheated oven, pour the reserved cupful of water onto the hot roasting pan and lower the oven temperature to 220°C (425°F) Gas 7.

14 Bake for about 12–15 minutes, or until golden brown. Don't worry if you see butter seeping out of the pains au chocolat during baking – it should all be absorbed when the pastries cool.

15 Let the pains au chocolat cool slightly on wire racks before eating.

A

B

C

PAINS AUX RAISINS

When you are expecting guests over the weekend, why not bake some of these irresistible *pains aux raisins* on Saturday, then warm them up for breakfast on Sunday morning? They will be appreciated so much more than a slice of toast or a storebought muffin.

1 quantity Croissant dough (see page 137, up to end of Step 25)

150 g/1 cup (dark) raisins

smooth apricot jam, for glazing

icing/confectioners' sugar, for glazing (optional)

CUSTARD

20 g/2½ tablespoons white plain/all-purpose flour

10 g/4 teaspoons cornflour/cornstarch

250 g/250 ml/1 cup whole milk

1 large egg, lightly beaten

50 g/¼ cup sugar

1 teaspoon vanilla extract

2 baking sheets lined with parchment paper

MAKES ABOUT 19

To make the custard

1 In a small mixing bowl, mix the flour and cornflour/cornstarch with about one quarter of the milk using a balloon whisk. Whisk until smooth.

2 Add the egg to the flour mixture.

3 In a saucepan, put the remaining milk, sugar and vanilla extract and heat until the sugar has dissolved and the mixture comes to a boil.

4 When it comes to a boil, add the flour mixture and whisk vigorously.

5 Keep whisking over the heat until it starts to thicken, then cook for a further 2 minutes.

6 Remove from the heat and transfer the custard to a bowl.

7 Place clingfilm/plastic wrap directly on top of the custard to prevent a skin from forming.

8 Let cool and refrigerate until needed.

9 The custard will keep, refrigerated, for 24 hours.

To make the pains aux raisins

1 Remove the croissant dough from the refrigerator and roll out to a rectangle about 24 x 38 cm/10 x 15 inches. **(A)**

2 Spread the custard on the dough using the back of a spoon. You may not need all the custard. **(B)**

3 Sprinkle the raisins evenly over the custard.

4 Now roll up the dough from a longer side to make a long log. **(C)**

5 Wrap the log in clingfilm/plastic wrap and refrigerate for 30 minutes.

6 Remove the dough from the refrigerator, discard the clingfilm/plastic wrap and cut the dough into roughly 2-cm/¾-inch slices. You should get about 19 slices. **(D)**

7 Lay each pastry flat on the prepared baking sheets. Tuck the end of each swirl of pastry underneath to help it retain its shape during baking. Allow a little space between them so that they have room to rise.

E

F

8 Let rise until you see the folds in the pastry separating. **(E)**

9 Preheat the oven to 240°C (475°F) Gas 9. Place a roasting pan at the bottom of the oven. Fill a cup with water.

10 Place the baking sheets in the preheated oven, pour the reserved cupful of water onto the hot roasting pan and lower the oven temperature to 220°C (425°F) Gas 7.

11 Bake for about 12–15 minutes, or until golden brown. Lower the oven temperature if it looks like the raisins are burning. And don't worry if you see butter seeping out of the pastries during baking – it should all be absorbed when the pastries cool.

12 While the pastries cool slightly, warm the apricot jam in a small saucepan.

13 Brush the warm jam over each warm pastry. **(F)**

14 To make an icing, if you like, mix a few tablespoons of icing/confectioners' sugar with a small amount of cold water in a small bowl. Add more water and stir until you have a smooth, runny consistency.

15 When the pastries are cold, drizzle the icing over them. **(G)**

G

A

B

C

D

COPENHAGENS

When I was an apprentice, we made these Danish-style pastries called Copenhagens. They are a sweet, fruity type of pastry bun with a hint of almonds and a very delicate flavour. They got me passionate about pastry. A word of warning! The folding technique is tricky, but practice makes perfect, so just be patient, follow the pictures and you will be rewarded.

1 quantity Croissant dough (see page 137, up to end of Step 25)

50 g/¼ cup smooth apricot jam, plus extra for glazing

100 g/¾ cup sultanas/golden raisins

icing/confectioners' sugar, for glazing (optional)

toasted flaked/slivered almonds, for sprinkling

FOR THE MARZIPAN FILLING

50 g/1¾ oz. good marzipan

50 g/3 tablespoons soft butter (salted or unsalted)

25 g/2 tablespoons caster/superfine sugar

1 medium egg

50 g/⅓ cup plus 1 tablespoon plain/all-purpose flour

2 baking sheets lined with parchment paper

MAKES ABOUT 11

To make the marzipan filling

1 Put the marzipan, soft butter and sugar in a small bowl.

2 Using a wooden spoon or a balloon whisk, beat until light and creamy.

3 Add the egg to the butter mixture and mix well.

4 Add the flour and mix until well combined.

5 You should have a thick paste.

6 Use the marzipan filling immediately. Alternatively, if you make it in advance, cover it with clingfilm/plastic wrap and refrigerate until needed. Bring it back to room temperature before using.

To make the Copenhagens

1 Remove the croissant dough from the refrigerator and roll out to a rectangle about 28 x 38 cm/ 11 x 15 inches.

2 Spread the apricot jam all over the rectangle of dough using the back of a spoon. **(A)**

3 Spread the marzipan filling (at room temperature) evenly over the layer of apricot jam using the back of the spoon again. Don't spread it right to the edges of the dough rectangle otherwise it will seep out when the dough is folded later. **(B)**

4 Sprinkle the sultanas/golden raisins evenly over a long edge of the dough, covering half of it. **(C)**

5 Fold the other long edge of the dough (without the sultanas/golden raisins) over the part covered in raisins.

6 Press lightly with your hands so that the 2 halves of the dough stick together.

7 Cut the dough into strips about 3.5 cm/1¼ inches wide. **(D)**

8 Take one strip and stretch it gently to lengthen it slightly. **(E)**

9 Follow the step-by-step photographs to the right to fold the Copenhagens in the right configuration. Gently stretch the dough to lengthen it, as you go. **(F) (G) (H) (I) (J)**

10 The finished shapes should be roughly circular, with no holes visible between the folds of dough. It will take practice to perfect this technique! **(K)**

11 Lay each pastry on the prepared baking sheets, making sure the ends are tucked in to help the pastry retain its shape during baking. Allow a little space between the pastries so that they have room to rise.

12 Let rise until you see the folds in the pastry separating. **(L)**

13 Preheat the oven to 240°C (475°F) Gas 9. Place a roasting pan at the bottom of the oven. Fill a cup with water.

14 Place the baking sheets in the preheated oven, pour the reserved cupful of water onto the hot roasting pan and lower the oven temperature to 220°C (425°F) Gas 7.

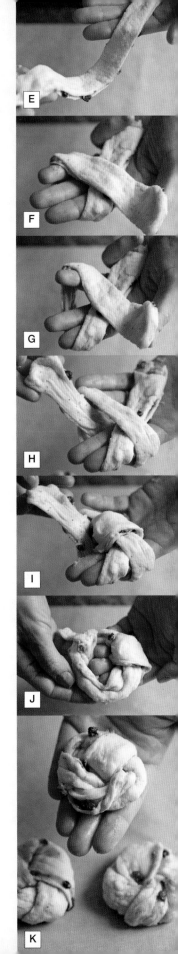

15 Bake the Copenhagens for about 12–15 minutes, or until golden brown. Don't worry if you see butter seeping out of the pastries during baking – it should all be absorbed when the pastries cool.

16 While the pastries cool slightly, warm the apricot jam in a small saucepan.

17 Brush the warm jam over each warm pastry. **(M)**

18 To make an icing, if you like, mix a few tablespoons of icing/confectioners' sugar with a small amount of cold water in a small bowl. Add more water and stir. Keep adding water, a little at a time, until the consistency is smooth and very runny.

19 Brush the icing roughly over the pastries. It will seep nicely into the cracks and folds of the Copenhagens. **(N)**

20 Sprinkle almonds over the top. **(O)**

21 Let the jam and icing set before serving.

L

BRIOCHE

This, like the previous recipes in this chapter, is another French classic. A good brioche, in my mind, is the perfect luxury. A subtly sweet bread enriched with egg and butter, it loves to be eaten with chocolate spread.

250 g/2 cups white strong/bread flour or French T55 flour

4 g/¾ teaspoon salt

30 g/2 tablespoons plus 1 teaspoon sugar

20 g fresh yeast or 10 g/1 tablespoon dried/active dry yeast

60 g/60 ml/¼ cup whole milk, warmed slightly

2 medium eggs

100 g/6½ tablespoons soft butter (salted or unsalted)

1 medium egg, beaten with a pinch of salt, for the egg wash

500-g/6 x 4-in. loaf pan, greased with butter

MAKES 1 SMALL LOAF

1 In one (smaller) mixing bowl, mix the flour, salt and sugar together and set aside. This is the dry mixture.

2 In a (larger) mixing bowl, weigh out the yeast. Add the milk and stir until the yeast has dissolved.

3 Lightly beat the eggs together, then add to the yeast solution. This is the wet mixture. **(A)**

4 Add the dry mixture to the wet mixture. **(B)**

5 Mix the mixtures together with your hands until it comes together. **(C)**

6 The mixture will be quite sticky. **(D)**

7 Cover with the bowl that had the dry mixture in it.

8 Let stand for 10 minutes.

9 After 10 minutes, knead as in Step 5 on page 87.

10 Cover the bowl again and let stand for a further 10 minutes.

11 Repeat Steps 9 and 10.

12 Pull small pieces off the butter and push into the dough. **(E)**

13 Knead the dough again to start incorporating the butter. Cover and let rise for 10 minutes.

14 Knead the dough for the last time and make sure that all the butter is fully incorporated. **(F)**

15 Cover, refrigerate and let rise for 1 hour. **(G)**

16 Punch down the dough.

17 Lightly dust a clean work surface with flour. Transfer the ball of dough to the floured work surface.

18 Divide the dough into 3 equal portions using a metal dough scraper or sharp, serrated knife. **(H)**

19 Take each portion of dough and roll between your hands until you get a perfectly round, smooth ball. **(I)**

20 Place the balls in the prepared loaf pan. **(J)**

21 Cover with a large bowl and let rise until slightly less than double the size – about 30–45 minutes.

22 About 20 minutes before baking, preheat the oven to 200°C (400°F) Gas 6. Place a roasting pan at the bottom of the oven to preheat. Fill a cup with water and set aside.

23 When the brioche has finished rising, brush it all over with the egg wash. **(K)**

24 Snip the top of each bump on the brioche with kitchen scissors. **(L)**

25 Place the brioche in the preheated oven and pour the reserved cupful of water onto the hot roasting pan.

26 Bake for about 20 minutes, or until golden brown.

27 To check if it is baked through, tip it upside down and tap the bottom – it should sound hollow. If it is ready, set it on a wire rack to cool.

E

F

G

H

A | B | C | D | E

CINNAMON ROLLS

These are a great complement to your morning coffee and ideal for sharing. I have made them in a cake pan so that they stay moist – simply pull them apart and enjoy. Cinnamon and coffee heaven!

5 g fresh yeast
or 3 g/1 teaspoon
dried/active dry yeast

20 g/2½ tablespoons
sugar, plus extra for
sprinkling

70 g/70 ml/5
tablespoons warm
water

100 g/¾ cup white
strong/bread flour

100 g/1 scant cup white
strong/bread flour

1 g/¼ teaspoon salt

1 teaspoon ground
cinnamon, plus extra
for sprinkling

1 medium egg, lightly
beaten

40 g/2½ tablespoons
soft butter (salted or
unsalted), plus extra,
melted, for brushing

1 medium egg, beaten
with a pinch of salt,
for the egg wash

icing/confectioners'
sugar, for dusting

*23-cm/9-in. round
cake pan, greased with
vegetable oil and lightly
dusted with flour*

MAKES ABOUT 13

1 In a (larger) mixing bowl, weigh out the yeast. Add the sugar and water and stir until the yeast and sugar have dissolved. Add the 100 g/¾ cup flour and mix with a wooden spoon until well mixed. This is the pre-ferment.

2 Cover and let ferment in a warm place until doubled in size – about 1 hour.

3 While the pre-ferment rises, in another (smaller) mixing bowl, mix the 100 g/1 scant cup flour, salt and cinnamon together. This is the dry mixture.

4 When the pre-ferment is ready, add the dry mixture and the egg and mix until it comes together.

5 Mix in the butter until well combined.

6 Cover and let stand for 10 minutes.

7 After 10 minutes, knead as in Step 5 on page 87.

8 Cover the bowl again and let stand for 10 minutes.

9 Repeat Steps 7 and 8 twice, then Step 7 again.

10 Cover the bowl and let rise for 1 hour.

11 When the dough has doubled in volume, punch it down with your fist to release the air.

12 Lightly dust a clean work surface with flour. Put the dough on the work surface.

13 Push the dough out with your fingertips to flatten it and widen it into a rectangle 3 mm/⅛ inch thick. **(A)**

14 Brush it all over with the egg wash. **(B)**

15 Sprinkle as much sugar and cinnamon as you like over the egg wash.

16 Now roll up the dough from a longer side to make a long log. **(C)**

17 Cut into roughly 2-cm/¾-inch slices. You should get about 13 slices. **(D)**

18 Arrange the slices, cut-side up, inside the prepared cake pan. They should fit quite snugly.

19 Cover and let rise until slightly less than double in size. **(E)**

20 About 20 minutes before baking, preheat the oven to 200°C (400°F) Gas 6. Place a roasting pan at the bottom of the oven to preheat. Fill a cup with water and set aside.

21 Place the cake pan in the preheated oven, pour the reserved cupful of water onto the hot roasting pan and lower the oven temperature to 180°C (350°F) Gas 4.

22 Bake the cinnamon rolls for about 10–15 minutes, or until golden brown.

23 Turn the rolls out onto a wire rack to cool.

24 Brush melted butter over the warm rolls and dust with icing/confectioners' sugar and ground cinnamon.

A | B | C

HOT CROSS BUNS

This is the traditional Easter treat in the UK. Start making these buns long before Easter if you like, because there's no reason they can't be enjoyed all year round. I love mine halved, toasted and dripping with melted butter.

FOR THE CROSSES
90 g/90 ml/⅓ cup water

40 g/40 ml/3 tablespoons vegetable oil

75 g/⅔ cup plain/all-purpose flour

2 g/½ teaspoon salt

FOR THE GLAZE
250 g/250 ml/1 cup water

150 g/¾ cup sugar

½ unwaxed orange, cut in 4

½ unwaxed lemon, cut in 2

2 cinnamon sticks

5 cloves

3 star anise

FOR THE DOUGH
10 g fresh yeast or 5 g/ 1½ teaspoons dried/active dry yeast

40 g/3 tablespoons sugar

200 g/200 ml/¾ cup warm water

200 g/1¾ cups plain/all-purpose flour

150 g/1 cup sultanas/golden raisins

150 g/1 cup (Zante) currants

1 teaspoon ground ginger

1 teaspoon ground cinnamon

¼ teaspoon ground cloves

grated zest of 2 unwaxed oranges

grated zest of 3 unwaxed lemons

200 g/1¾ cups white strong/ bread flour

2 g/½ teaspoon salt

90 g/6 tablespoons soft butter (salted or unsalted)

1 large egg, lightly beaten

baking sheet lined with parchment paper

piping bag fitted with a small plain nozzle/tip

MAKES 15

To make the mixture for the crosses

1 Mix the water and oil together in a measuring cup or similar.

2 In a small bowl, mix the flour and salt together. **(A)**

3 Add the oil mixture to the flour and salt mixture and mix with a wooden spoon until you get a soft, smooth paste. **(B)**

4 Cover and set aside in a cool place until needed.

To make the glaze

1 Put the water, sugar, orange, lemon, cinnamon, cloves and star anise in a saucepan and heat. Bring to a boil.

2 When the liquid comes to a boil, take off the heat and set aside in a cool place to allow the spices and citrus to infuse. **(C)**

3 This glaze can be made a day in advance and stored in the refrigerator to use repeatedly for this recipe.

D

E

F

To make the dough

1 In a (larger) mixing bowl, weigh out the yeast. Add the sugar and water and stir until the yeast and sugar have dissolved. Add the plain/all-purpose flour and mix with a wooden spoon until well mixed. This is the pre-ferment. **(D) (E)**

2 Cover the bowl and let ferment in a warm place until doubled in size – about 30 minutes. **(F)**

3 While the pre-ferment rises, weigh out the dried fruit, spices and zest, mix together and set aside. **(G)**

4 In another (smaller) mixing bowl, mix the strong/bread flour and salt together. This is the dry mixture.

5 Pull small pieces off the butter and lightly rub into the dry mixture using your fingertips until there are no more big lumps of butter. **(H) (I)**

6 After 30 minutes, the pre-ferment will have risen quite a bit.

7 Add the egg and pre-ferment to the flour mixture and mix with your hands until it comes together. **(J) (K)**

G

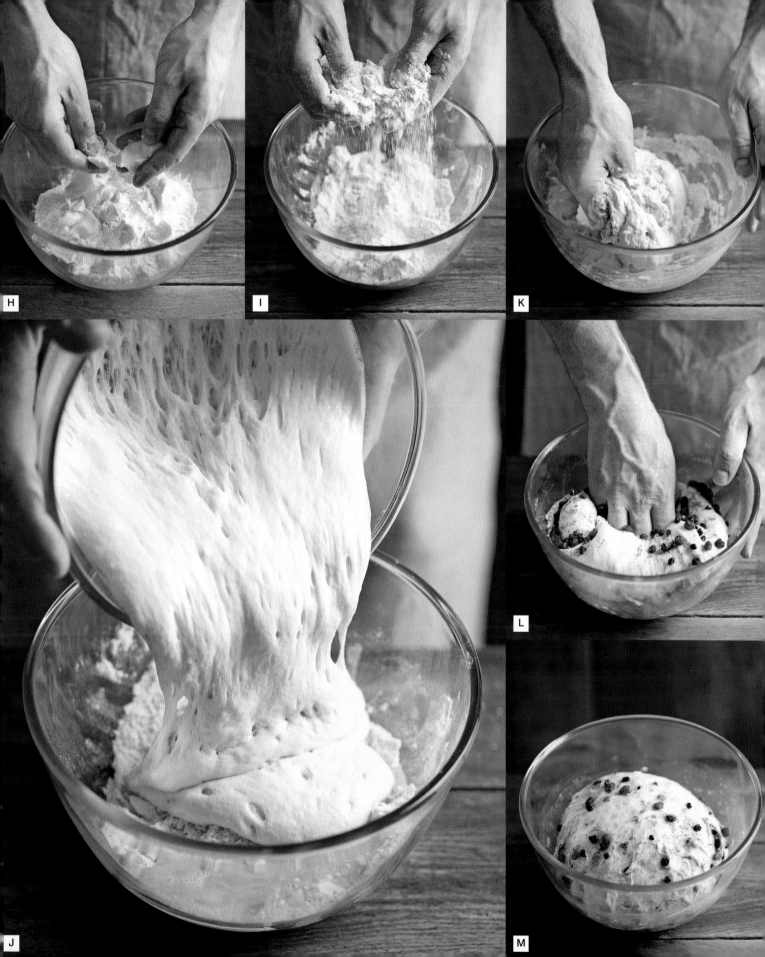

N

O

P

Q

R

S

8 Cover and let stand for 10 minutes.

9 After 10 minutes, knead as in Step 5 on page 87.

10 Cover the bowl again and let stand for 10 minutes.

11 Repeat Steps 9 and 10 three times.

12 Add the reserved dried fruit mixture to the dough and knead gently until thoroughly mixed in. **(L)**

13 Cover and let rise for 30 minutes. **(M)**

14 At this this stage, you can refrigerate the dough and continue the recipe the next day, if necessary. In this case, let the dough sit at room temperature for about 15 minutes before continuing.

15 Lightly dust a clean work surface with flour.

16 Transfer the dough to the floured work surface.

17 After 30 minutes, divide the dough into 15 equal portions using a metal dough scraper or sharp, serrated knife. **(N)**

18 Each portion should weigh about 70 g/2½ oz. If you want to be as accurate as possible, weigh each piece and add or subtract dough from the portions until they all weigh the same. **(O)**

19 Take one portion of dough and roll between your hands until you get a perfectly round ball. Put on the prepared baking sheet. Repeat with the remaining dough. Allow a little space between them so that they have room to rise and arrange them in neat rows and lines. **(P)**

20 Cover and let rise until about double the size. **(Q)**

21 About 20 minutes before baking, preheat the oven to 220°C (425°F) Gas 7. Place a roasting pan at the bottom of the oven to preheat. Fill a cup with water and set aside.

22 Fill a piping bag with the reserved mixture for the crosses. Pipe continuous lines across the tops of the buns in both directions. **(R)**

23 Place the baking sheet in the preheated oven, pour the reserved cupful of water onto the hot roasting pan and lower the oven temperature to 180°C (350°F) Gas 4.

24 Bake for about 10–15 minutes, or until golden brown.

25 Remove from the oven. Brush lightly with the cold, reserved glaze. **(S)**

26 Allow to cool on the tray and serve.

MARZIPAN STOLLEN

Christmas is not the same without some kind of fruit cake. In Germany, they have Stollen, with marzipan in the middle. We at Judges were lucky to win first prize at the Brockwell Bake and a Gold in The Great Taste Awards for this Stollen. I am very passionate about this bread, as I learned how to make it from a master baker and confectioner in Münster, Germany.

A

B

C

D

100 g/3½ oz. good marzipan

vanilla sugar, to taste

icing/confectioners' sugar, for dusting

FOR THE FRUIT MIXTURE

60 g/½ cup sultanas/golden raisins

15 g/2 tablespoons toasted flaked/slivered almonds

15 g/1 generous tablespoon diced candied citrus peel

freshly squeezed juice and grated zest of 1 small unwaxed orange

freshly squeezed juice and grated zest of 1 unwaxed lemon

15 g/15 ml/1 tablespoon rum

FOR THE DOUGH

10 g fresh yeast or 5 g/1½ teaspoons dried/active dry yeast

20 g/20 ml/4 teaspoons whole milk, warmed

20 g/2½ tablespoons white strong/bread flour

50 g/3 tablespoons plus 1 teaspoon soft butter (salted or unsalted)

20 g/2 tablespoons sugar

1 g/¼ teaspoon salt

1 g/¼ teaspoon ground cardamom

¼ teaspoon vanilla extract

1 medium egg, beaten

150 g/1¼ cups white strong/bread flour

150 g/10 tablespoons butter (salted or unsalted), melted

FOR THE GLAZE

30 g/¼ cup smooth apricot jam

45 g/3 tablespoons butter (salted or unsalted)

30 g/2 tablespoons sugar

1 tablespoon whole milk

baking sheet lined with parchment paper

MAKES 1 MEDIUM STOLLEN

To make the fruit mixture (one week in advance)

1 In a large mixing bowl, mix together all the ingredients.

2 Cover the bowl with clingfilm/plastic wrap and let stand in a cool place for up to 1 week. When it is ready, most of the liquid should have been absorbed.

To make the dough

1 In a (larger) mixing bowl, weigh out the yeast. Add the milk and stir until the yeast has dissolved. **(A)**

2 Add the 20 g/2½ tablespoons flour and mix with a wooden spoon until well mixed. This is the pre-ferment. **(B)**

3 Cover the bowl and let ferment in a warm place until doubled in size – about 30 minutes.

4 While the pre-ferment rises, in another (smaller) mixing bowl, beat the 50 g/3 tablespoons plus 1 teaspoon butter, sugar, salt, cardamom and vanilla extract with a balloon whisk until soft. **(C)**

5 Add the egg, little by little, whisking well. **(D)**

6 If the mixture separates, add a teaspoon of flour (from the 150 g/1¼ cups) to help bind it.

7 Mix about 1 tablespoon of the flour (from the 150 g/1¼ cups) into the reserved fruit mixture to absorb any surplus moisture. Set aside.

8 When the pre-ferment has risen, stir it into the butter mixture.

9 Add the remaining 150 g/1¼ cups flour to the mixture and mix until it comes together.

10 Cover and let stand for 10 minutes.

11 After 10 minutes, knead as in Step 5 on page 87.

12 Cover the bowl again and let stand for 10 minutes.

13 Repeat Steps 11 and 12 three times. **(E)**

14 Add the reserved dried fruit mixture to the dough and knead gently until thoroughly mixed in.

15 Cover and let rise until about double the size – about 1 hour. **(F)**

16 Lightly dust a clean work surface with flour.

17 Punch down the dough to release the air and transfer to the floured work surface.

18 Shape the dough into a ball and let rest until it is workable – about 5 minutes.

19 Meanwhile, shape the marzipan into a short sausage.

E

F

G

H

I

J

K

L

20 Dust the dough with a little flour so that it does not stick to the rolling pin. Roll out the dough to a rough square. **(G)**

21 Place the marzipan sausage in the middle. **(H)**

22 Pull the dough over the ends of the marzipan. **(I)**

23 Fold the side closest to you over the marzipan to enclose it completely. **(J)**

24 Fold the side furthest from you over. **(K)**

25 Roll the Stollen over so that the seam is underneath. Use both hands to mould the dough around the marzipan in the middle. **(L)**

26 Transfer the Stollen to the prepared baking sheet, cover and let rise in a warm place until slightly less than double the size – about 30 minutes. **(M)**

27 About 20 minutes before baking, preheat the oven to 200°C (400°F) Gas 6. Place a roasting pan at the bottom of the oven to preheat. Fill a cup with water and set aside.

28 Place the baking sheet in the preheated oven, pour the reserved cupful of water onto the hot roasting pan and lower the oven temperature to 180°C (350°F) Gas 4.

29 Bake for about 20 minutes, or until golden brown.

30 To check if it is baked through, tip it upside down and tap the bottom – it should sound hollow. If it is not ready, return to the oven for a few minutes.

31 Dislodge any darkened raisins stuck to the baking sheet with a sharp knife, but take care not to damage the Stollen.

32 Brush the Stollen with the hot, melted butter, allow to seep into the dough, then repeat twice more. **(N)**

33 Let cool completely.

To make the glaze and finish the Stollen

1 Put the ingredients for the glaze in a pan and bring to a boil.

2 Brush the glaze all over (top and bottom) the cold Stollen.

3 Generously dust a tray with vanilla sugar and put the freshly glazed Stollen on it. Dust the top and sides with the vanilla sugar, too. **(O)**

4 Finally, dust the Stollen with icing/confectioners' sugar. **(P)**

POPPYSEED STOLLEN

I love marzipan Stollen, but a Stollen made with poppyseeds stands out just as much. The seeds become very sticky and create a beautiful pattern through the middle of the bread. This makes a lovely addition to a Christmas table.

vanilla sugar, to taste

icing/confectioners' sugar, for dusting

FOR THE POPPYSEED FILLING

100 g/6 tablespoons poppyseeds

30 g/2 tablespoons melted butter

2 tablespoons honey

1 medium egg

50 g/4 tablespoons sultanas/golden raisins

50 g/¼ cup fine semolina

20 g/2 teaspoons sugar

FOR THE DOUGH

10 g fresh yeast or 5 g/1½ teaspoons dried/active dry yeast

20 g/20 ml/4 teaspoons whole milk, warmed

20 g/2½ tablespoons white strong/bread flour

50 g/3 tablespoons plus 1 teaspoon soft butter (salted or unsalted)

20 g/2 tablespoons sugar

1 g/¼ teaspoon salt

1 g/¼ teaspoon ground cardamom

¼ teaspoon vanilla extract

1 medium egg, beaten

150 g/1¼ cups white strong/ bread flour

100 g/6½ tablespoons butter (salted or unsalted), melted

FOR THE GLAZE

30 g/¼ cup smooth apricot jam

45 g/3 tablespoons butter (salted or unsalted)

30 g/2 tablespoons sugar

1 tablespoon whole milk

900-g/8½ x 4½-in. loaf pan, greased with vegetable oil

MAKES 1 LARGE STOLLEN

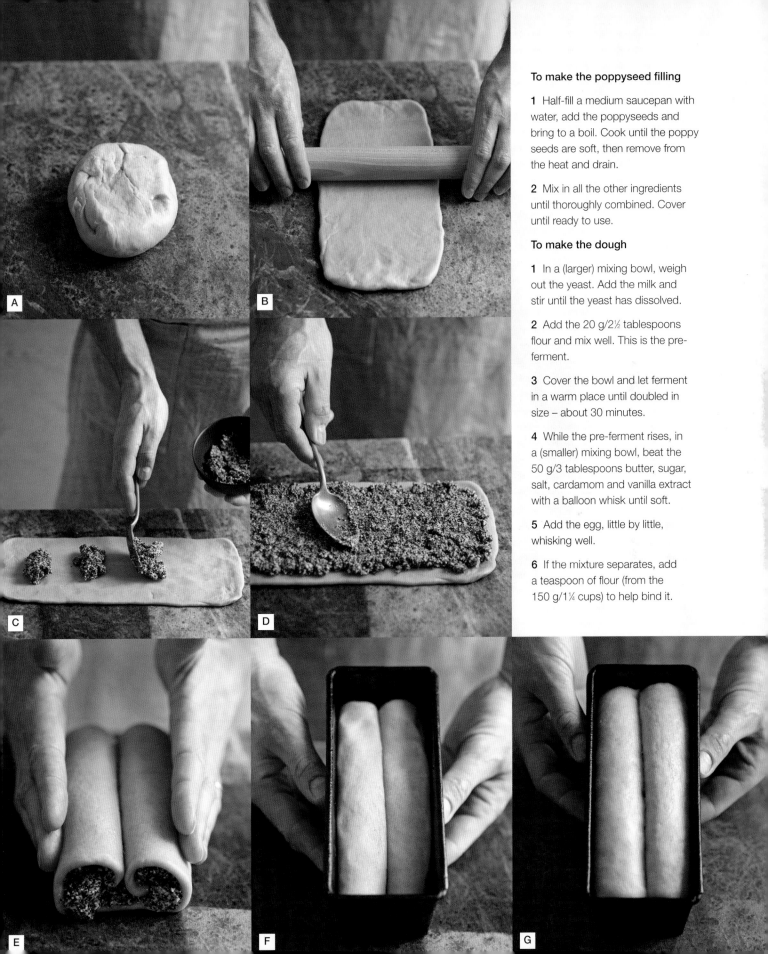

A

B

C

D

To make the poppyseed filling

1 Half-fill a medium saucepan with water, add the poppyseeds and bring to a boil. Cook until the poppy seeds are soft, then remove from the heat and drain.

2 Mix in all the other ingredients until thoroughly combined. Cover until ready to use.

To make the dough

1 In a (larger) mixing bowl, weigh out the yeast. Add the milk and stir until the yeast has dissolved.

2 Add the 20 g/2½ tablespoons flour and mix well. This is the pre-ferment.

3 Cover the bowl and let ferment in a warm place until doubled in size – about 30 minutes.

4 While the pre-ferment rises, in a (smaller) mixing bowl, beat the 50 g/3 tablespoons butter, sugar, salt, cardamom and vanilla extract with a balloon whisk until soft.

5 Add the egg, little by little, whisking well.

6 If the mixture separates, add a teaspoon of flour (from the 150 g/1¼ cups) to help bind it.

E

F

G

H

I

7 When the pre-ferment has risen, stir it into the butter mixture. Add the remaining 150 g/1¼ cups flour and mix until it comes together. Cover and let stand for 10 minutes.

8 After 10 minutes, knead as in Step 5 on page 87.

9 Cover the bowl again and let stand for 10 minutes.

10 Repeat Steps 8 and 9 twice, then Step 8 again.

11 Cover and let rise until about double the size – about 1 hour.

12 Punch down the dough and transfer to the work surface. Shape into a ball and let rest until workable – about 5 minutes. **(A)**

13 Roll the dough out with a rolling pin into a rectangle 21 x 37 cm /8½ x 15 inches, or no wider than the length of your loaf pan. **(B)**

14 Spoon the poppyseed filling onto the dough and spread evenly with the back of the spoon. **(C) (D)**

15 Roll one short side of the dough toward the middle, then repeat with the other side to make a pinwheel. **(E)**

16 Place carefully inside the prepared loaf pan. **(F)**

17 Cover and let rise in a warm place until slightly less than double the size – about 30 minutes. **(G)**

18 About 20 minutes before baking, preheat the oven to 200°C (400°F) Gas 6. Place a roasting pan at the bottom of the oven to preheat. Fill a cup with water and set aside.

19 Place the loaf pan in the preheated oven, pour the reserved cupful of water onto the hot roasting pan and lower the oven temperature to 180°C (350°F) Gas 4.

20 Bake for about 20 minutes, or until golden brown. **(H)**

21 To check if it is baked through, tip it upside down and tap the bottom – it should sound hollow. If it is not ready, return to the oven for a few minutes.

22 Remove the Stollen from the pan. Brush with the hot, melted butter and allow to seep into the dough, then repeat twice more.

23 Let cool completely.

To make the glaze and finish the Stollen

1 Put the ingredients for the glaze in a pan and bring to a boil.

2 Brush the glaze all over (top and bottom) the cold Stollen.

3 Dust a tray with vanilla sugar and put the freshly glazed Stollen on it. Dust the top and sides with the vanilla sugar, too. Finally, dust with icing/confectioners' sugar. **(I)**

SUPPLIERS & STOCKISTS

UK

Fresh yeast can be bought from bakeries and most supermarkets with in-store bakeries.

Shipton Mill
Long Newnton
Tetbury
Gloucestershire GL8 8RP
Te: +44 (0)1666 505050
www.shipton-mill.com
For many, many types of organic flour, milled on site, available to buy online in small or large quantities. Find the wheatgerm and bran mixture here, as used in the Wholegrain Sourdough on page 92. They also stock proofing/dough-rising baskets. Their website is also a good reference for the mechanics of flour and grains.

Doves Farm
Doves Farm Foods Ltd
Salisbury Road
Hungerford
Berkshire RG17 0RF
Tel: +44 (0)1488 684880
www.dovesfarm.co.uk
Like Shipton Mill, Doves Farm supplies many, many types of organic flour, milled on site and available to buy online in small or large quantities, as well as all sorts of other organic products. They stock a large range of proofing/dough-rising baskets in all sizes and shapes

Athenian Grocery
16A Moscow Road
Bayswater
London W2 4BT
Tel: +44 (0)20 7229 6280
For the mahlepi/mahleb (ground black cherry pit) used in the Tsoureki recipe on page 55.

The Spice Shop
1 Blenheim Crescent
London W11 2EE
Tel: +44 (0)207 221 4448
www.thespiceshop.co.uk
For every kind of spice under the sun.

www.brotformen.de
Tel: +49 (0)34 364 522 87
German supplier of proofing/dough-rising baskets in all manner of shapes and sizes.

Bakery Bits
1 Orchard Units, Duchy Road
Honiton
Devon EX14 1YD
Tel: +44 (0)1404 565656
www.bakerybits.co.uk
Online supplier of every kind of tool, utensil and equipment needed to bake bread.

Lakeland
Tel: +44 (0)1539 488100
www.lakeland.co.uk
Stockists of bakeware and cookware, with branches around the UK, as well as an excellent website.

Divertimenti
Tel: +44 (0)870 129 5026
www.divertimenti.co.uk
Cookware stockist, with branches in London and Cambridge, as well as an online store.

Nisbets
Tel: +44 (0)845 140 5555
www.nisbets.co.uk
Enormous range of catering equipment to buy online, including loaf pans and more, plus branches in London and Bristol.

The Traditional Cornmillers Guild
www.tcmg.org.uk
For details of individual mills around the UK.

US

King Arthur Flour
Tel: +1 800 827 6836
www.kingarthurflour.com
America's oldest – and one of the best – flour company. Flours are unbleached and never bromated. Their great selection of flours includes 9-grain flour blend, malted wheat flakes, Irish-style wholemeal flour, French-style flour for baguettes, European-style artisan bread flour, as well as sugar, yeast in bulk, sourdough starters, baking pans, /proofing dough-rising baskets, bread/pizza peels and other bakeware and equipment

Bob's Red Mill
Tel: +1 (503) 654 3215
www.bobsredmill.com
Online supplier of traditional and gluten-free flours, plus grains and seeds.

Hodgson Mill
Tel: +1 800 347 0105
www.hodgsonmill.com
Suppliers of all-natural, whole grains and stoneground products.

Penzeys Spices
Tel: +1 800 741 7787
www.penzeys.com
Suppliers of pink peppercorns, vanilla, cardamom, cinnamon, star anise and more.

Kalustyan's Spices and Sweets
Tel: +1 800 352 2451
www.kalustyans.com
Dried fruits, nuts and spices, including the mahlepi/mahleb (ground black cherry pit) used in the Tsoureki recipe on page 55.

Breadtopia
Tel: +1 800 469 7989
www.breadtopia.com
From dough scrapers to rising baskets, and sourdough starters, this Iowa-based company has every gadget and pan an artisan bread baker could ever want.

La Cuisine – The Cook's Resource
Tel: +1 800 521 1176
www.lacuisineus.com
Fine bakeware including oval and round prroofing/dough-rising baskets, loaf pans in every size and bread/pizza peels.

Crate & Barrel
Tel: +1 630 369 4464
www.crateandbarrel.com
Good stockist of bakeware online and in stores throughout the country.

Sur la table
Tel: +1 800 243 0852
www.surlatable.com
Good stockist of bakeware online and in stores throughout the country.

Williams-Sonoma
Tel: +1 877 812 6235
www.williams-sonoma.com
Good stockist of bakeware online and in stores throughout the country.

INDEX

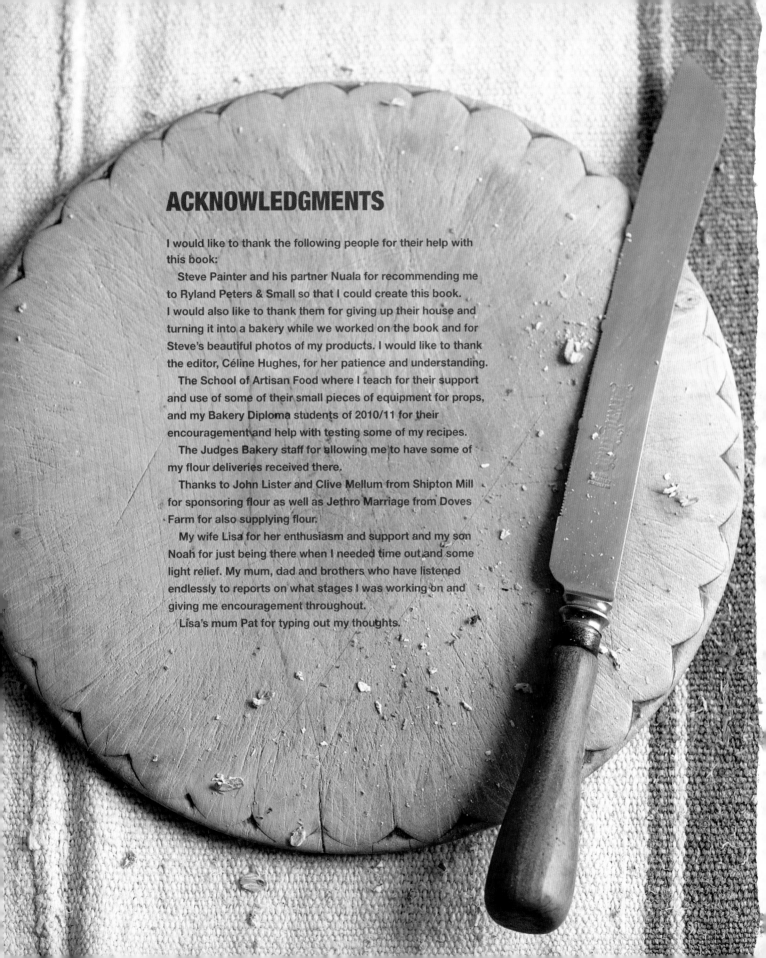

ACKNOWLEDGMENTS

I would like to thank the following people for their help with this book:

Steve Painter and his partner Nuala for recommending me to Ryland Peters & Small so that I could create this book. I would also like to thank them for giving up their house and turning it into a bakery while we worked on the book and for Steve's beautiful photos of my products. I would like to thank the editor, Céline Hughes, for her patience and understanding.

The School of Artisan Food where I teach for their support and use of some of their small pieces of equipment for props, and my Bakery Diploma students of 2010/11 for their encouragement and help with testing some of my recipes.

The Judges Bakery staff for allowing me to have some of my flour deliveries received there.

Thanks to John Lister and Clive Mellum from Shipton Mill for sponsoring flour as well as Jethro Marriage from Doves Farm for also supplying flour.

My wife Lisa for her enthusiasm and support and my son Noah for just being there when I needed time out and some light relief. My mum, dad and brothers who have listened endlessly to reports on what stages I was working on and giving me encouragement throughout.

Lisa's mum Pat for typing out my thoughts.